WRITE FROM THE START

David M. Davidson
Bronx Community College
City University of New York

David Blot
Hostos Community College
City University of New York

HEINLE & HEINLE PUBLISHERS
A Division of Wadsworth, Inc.
Boston, Massachusetts 02116

Library of Congress Cataloging in Publication Data

Davidson, David M.
    Write from the start.

    1. English language--Text-books for foreign speakers.
2. English language--Composition and exercises.
I. Blot, Dave. II. Title.
PE1128.D348   1984   808'.042   83-22075

Cover design by Barbara Frake
Cartoons by Richard Noyes

First printing: February 1984
Printed in the U.S.A.
14 15

To
Daniel Philip *and* Carmela

ACKNOWLEDGMENTS

With appreciation to our students for their encouraging response to this book; to Irene Dutra and Elizabeth Lara for their helpful suggestions; and with special thanks to Evangeline Caliandro for allowing us to include Picture Story 1.

INTRODUCTION

This book is based on the following principles, which stem from our experience teaching adult learners and from our training in the Counseling-Learning/ Community Language Learning approach to teaching languages.

1. Beginning adult ESL learners can write English, given proper guidance and security.
2. In most instances, students should have the opportunity to express their ideas orally before writing them.
3. Students will be more willing to express themselves through speaking and writing (i.e., to take the risks involved) if they really *want* to communicate.
4. Once they have invested themselves in communicating, through writing they are ready and motivated to learn the technicalities, i.e., grammar, spelling, and so on.

Therefore, this book attempts to provide activities

1. that immediately engage students in speaking and writing,
2. that are both controlled enough to provide security and interesting enough for adults to want to be bothered with,
3. that encourage student interaction, and
4. that provide experience and practice in the basics of English.

Write from the Start is divided into eight sections. The first, **Starting to Write**, is intended as the jumping-off point. It is the heart of the book, providing control, guidance, security, and the opportunity for students to talk and write about themselves, their friends, their relatives, and their ideas.

In the last section, **Exercising**, we employ a format we have found useful in giving students practice in some of the basics. This section is placed last because we feel it should be used after students have attempted to function in the language and after the teacher has responded to their interests and needs by teaching discrete grammatical points. Students will learn to write by writing. The teaching will be more appropriate and effective when it responds to the needs of the students as they perceive them through their desire to communicate effectively.

Activities from the six sections in between are intended to be used interchangeably at the instructor's discretion, depending upon the students' level, rate of progress, and needs.

We intend this book to be interesting and fun for both students and teachers, the kind of textbook that people want to turn to. If our intention has been realized, students will learn from it and teachers will enjoy helping them use it.

THE SECTIONS

Starting to Write is composed of three different types of exercises organized by tense in order of difficulty. The simplest type of exercise is the *model composition* (*My Classmate, About Me* and *A Good Friend* in the present tense, *My Parents* and *More about Me* in the past tense, and *A Letter* in the present continuous). Students begin the activity by reading the questions to themselves and asking for help as they need it from the instructor or the other students. Then, in pairs or in small groups, they should ask each other the questions and take notes (where appropriate). They will then be asked to read the model composition (aloud or to themselves) and to write. The model provides considerable security in the form of structure and vocabulary for those who need it. Such students may need to copy the composition and substitute appropriate information. Those who have the ability to write without copying, or even without using the model, should be encouraged to do so.

The second type of exercise in this section asks students to move from *an oral to a writing activity.* (*Twins* and *The Storekeeper* in the present and *The Park, An Evening Out, The Phone Call, The Test, The First Day of English Class* in the past.) The questions on the left-hand page are intended for oral use by students in pairs or groups. They may differ somewhat from the questions on the right-hand page which are intended to elicit a written response. Their purpose is to have students think and talk about the topic in general before getting to writing the specifics. For example, in *The Phone Call* the questions, "Do you like to receive phone calls?" and "If someone calls you and you don't want to talk to that person, what do you do?" are intended to generate thought and discussion about a common experience before getting the students to talk and then write about a specific illustrative incident. The questions on the right-hand page provide considerable security for those who need it. Students may choose from among the possibilities offered or supply their own information. Again, those with more facility should be encouraged to write their own stories, using the questions only as an outline.

All of the remaining activities in this section call for *responses to questions,* some highly structured with choices, some more open-ended. Most of them suggest beginning with a discussion which in most cases is about a third person— friend, teacher, parent, or relative. These exercises tend to be longer, offer some guidance as to paragraph division, and some involve writing in more than one tense. Where the person is imaginary (e.g., Donald in *A Vacation,* Nancy in *The Doctor,* and Peter in *A Decision*) the partners must agree on the details to be written.

This first section, along with the exercise work in the back and any supplementary work and instruction provided by the teacher, could well compose a third to a half or more of a semester's work, depending upon the level and rate of development of the students. Where some students develop their writing ability at a much faster pace than others, they of course may be encouraged to move ahead in the book to the other sections.

The order of exercises in this section does not necessarily suggest the teacher's order of presentation. For example, many teachers prefer to begin with the past tense, and it is often useful to return to a tense exercise for review.

All of the exercises in **Interacting** are orally based and intended to be used that way, with writing as a follow-up. They focus on questioning and giving directions, two of the most common elements in everyday conversation. They will all need demonstration, and we have found it useful for the instructor to work with one volunteer student in front of the class with the written follow-up placed on the board. After one or two examples, two students might be asked to demonstrate for the class before everyone begins. Because the instructions are complicated, particularly in *Compatibility Quotient* and *Taking Messages,* the instructor will need to supervise. Instructors will find that the students will have difficulty forming certain questions for the *Student Interview* because of such constructions as "Date of Arrival in the U.S." and "Reasons for. . . ." These were included because they are realistic kinds of items students may very well have to deal with outside the classroom. When students manifest difficulty with these items, the instructor can appropriately "teach"—to an individual, to groups, or to the whole class as appropriate.

Aside from being fun, the **Filling In** exercises are designed to give students some awareness of grammatical forms and sentence structure as well as some vocabulary extension. The word selection part of the activity is excellent for group work, while the follow-up copying and/or writing is an individual activity. In the former, any choice of words or phrases should be acceptable if they are grammatically and semantically appropriate to the context.

In our first book for more advanced students, *Put It In Writing,* we found dialogue activities to be very popular with students because the situations involved them in realistic conflicts they could identify with, yet permitted them the distance and security of role-playing. The dialogue situations in **Talking It Over** are intended to be fairly common experiences which nevertheless generate emotion and which can be dealt with in relatively simple, familiar language. Once again, this is the type of exercise that should be demonstrated by a dialogue either between a teacher and a student or between two students. (In pairing students for this activity we found that, as a rule, women feel more comfortable playing male roles than vice versa, so dialogues calling for male-female interaction should be conducted by a male and a female or by two females. Of course, you can change the gender of a character, if you feel that is more appropriate.)

In **Telling Stories** students are given the opportunity to write in more than one tense or to choose between present and past. The directions are clear, and once again we urge that discussion precede writing.

Students must write in the past tense to complete the stories in **Putting an End to It**. The person and tone vary from story to story however, providing the opportunity for a range of writing experiences.

Keeping It Personal means just that. We do not ask or expect students to talk about beforehand or share afterward their thoughts on these matters. Our experience is, however, that students often do want to share these personal thoughts with us. This section, in fact, was inspired by many of our students who have spontaneously showed us personal unassigned writing of this type. In this case we feel the instructor's response should be an encouraging one, concerned more with content than with form.

As we stated earlier, "teaching" should follow "doing," and so we regard the **Exercising** section as supplementary to the writing activities in the rest of the book. We chose the fill-in story format because it allows students to practice major grammatical points while building a story. In some cases material from other sections has been reworked here; e.g., *Moneybags, The Time Machine, About Me,* and *Caught in the Act.* Where appropriate, students might follow up the writing exercise with the grammar exercise and check the results themselves. In the other format we use in this section, students must produce questions for given answers.

Walk the students through a couple of the earlier exercises, especially the *questions for answers.* Having to provide questions for answers, the reverse of the normal language function, will require patient training at first. But after a few exercises, most students will understand how to do it. We have found this format, in spite of its unnaturalness, to be highly stimulating—an effective teaching device that helps students make connections between the wording of questions and answers and that forces them to respond to the content of the accompanying stories.

We have enjoyed writing this book, and our students have enjoyed using it while making significant and satisfying progress in developing their language skills. We hope you and your students have similar experiences and we invite you to share them with us.

David M. Davidson
David Blot

CONTENTS

STARTING TO WRITE

MY CLASSMATE

ACTIVITY   Get to know your classmate. Ask your classmate the questions below. Write the answers on a piece of paper. Then your classmate will ask you the questions and will write the answers.

1. What is your name?
2. Where are you from?
3. How old are you?
4. Where do you live?
5. Who do you live with?
6. Do you have any brothers and sisters?
7. Are you married?
8. Do you have any children?
9. Why are you studying English?
10. What do you like to do in your free time?

Now write a paragraph about your classmate. First read the paragraph below. You may use it as a model if you want to.

My Classmate

My classmate's name is Elizabeth. She is from Greece. She is 22 years old. She lives in Westwood with her mother, father and three sisters. Elizabeth is not married. She doesn't have any children, but she wants to have a son and a daughter. She is studying English because she wants to be a computer programmer. In her free time Elizabeth likes to play tennis, read good books and go out with her friends. She wants me to play tennis with her on Saturday. I'm happy that Elizabeth is my classmate.

ABOUT ME

ACTIVITY   Choose someone in the class that you don't know very well. Ask this person the following questions and then he/she will ask you the questions.

1. What is your name?
2. How old are you?
3. Where do you come from?
4. Where do you live?
5. Who do you live with?
6. Are your parents and brothers and sisters here or in your native country?
7. What is your major subject in school?
   or
   What kind of job do you have?
8. What do you want to become?
9. What are your hobbies?
10. Is there anything else you want to tell about yourself?

Now write a paragraph about yourself. First read the paragraph below. You may use it as a model if you want to.

About Me

My name is Tom. I am 23 years old. I come from Cambodia. I live at 193 Union Avenue. I live with my brother and his wife. My parents are in Cambodia. I have another brother and two sisters in Cambodia, also. My major subject is Electrical Technology. I want to become an engineer. My hobbies are dancing and going to the movies. After I finish my education, I want to get a good job. I also want to get married and have children.

A GOOD FRIEND

ACTIVITY Ask your partner or someone in your group these questions. Then your partner or someone in your group will ask you the questions.

1. What is your friend's name?
2. What nationality is your friend?
3. How old is your friend?
4. How tall is your friend?
5. How much does your friend weigh?
6. What color is your friend's hair?
7. What color are your friend's eyes?
8. Is your friend's complexion light or dark?
9. What does your friend usually wear?
10. Is your friend intelligent? Understanding? Generous?
11. Does your friend have a good sense of humor?
12. What is the most important thing you want to tell about your friend?

Now write a paragraph about your friend. First read the paragraph below. You may use it as a model if you want to.

A Good Friend

My friend's name is Marie. She is Haitian. She is 20 years old. Marie is 5'3" tall and weighs about 110 pounds. Her hair is black and her eyes are brown. She has a dark complexion. She usually wears a skirt and sweater to school. She wears jeans at home. Marie is very intelligent and very understanding. She has a good sense of humor. She always laughs at my jokes. Marie is a good athlete. She likes sports. She also likes music and children. We get along very well together.

TWINS

ACTIVITY Ask your partner or someone in your group these questions. Then your partner or someone in your group will ask you the questions.

1. Have you ever met twins? What are their names?

2. Do they look exactly alike or can you tell them apart? Explain.

3. Do they behave the same or differently? Give examples.

4. Do they like each other or do they fight a lot?

5. Do (Did) their parents treat them differently?

6. Would you like to be a twin? Why?

7. If you had twins, how would you treat them?

TWINS

ACTIVITY   Write a story about the twins, Ana and Maria.

Do Ana and Maria look *exactly like each other?*
a little like each other?
different from each other?

Are they *children?*
teen-agers?
adults?

_____?

Do they live *with their parents?*
with their husbands and children?
alone?

_____?

Do they *go to school?*
work?

_____?

Do they like the same *clothes?*
games?
books?
friends?

_____?

Do they like *to dance?*
to go to the movies?
to watch television?

_____?

Are they *funny?*
interesting?
selfish?
generous?

_____?

Are they good to *their parents?*
each other?
their children?

_____?

Are they *happy being twins?*
unhappy being twins?

THE STOREKEEPER

ACTIVITY Ask your partner or someone in your group these questions. Then your partner or someone in your group will ask you the questions.

1. Do you shop in a small store in your neighborhood? What kind of store is it?

2. What do you usually buy there?

3. Where is it located?

4. Why do you like to go there? Is it convenient? Inexpensive? Open early or late?

5. What kind of person is the storekeeper? Is he or she friendly? Courteous? Generous? Bad-tempered? Neat? Sloppy?

6. Do you like him or her? Why?

THE STOREKEEPER

ACTIVITY   Write a story about Mr. Caruso. Write three paragraphs.

1st para.

Is Mr. Caruso the storekeeper of *a grocery store?*
a candy store?
a discount store?

a _____?

Is the store *across the street from the movie theater?*
next to the post office?
around the corner from the dry cleaners?

_____?

Does Mr. Caruso open his store every morning *at 7:00?*
at 8:00?
at 9:00?

at _____?

Does he get everything ready for business?

Then does he begin to wait on the customers?

2nd. para.

Do many people come to his store every day?

Do they shop there *because it is convenient?*
because his prices are reasonable?
because it is the only store nearby?

because _____?

Do the customers like Mr. Caruso? Why or why not?

3rd para.

Does Mr. Caruso close his store *at 5:00?*
at 6:00?
at 9:30?

at _____?

Does he go home *very happy?*
very tired?
very sleepy?

very _____?   } **Why?**

9

A VACATION

ACTIVITY   Donald is a friend of yours. With your partner, talk about Donald's vacation. Using the choices you are given, you and your partner decide what you want to write. Then write three paragraphs. Each of you write on your own paper.

1st para.

Does Donald take his vacation in *July* every year?
August
December

_____

Does he usually go to *Hawaii*?
Puerto Rico?
France?

_____ ?

Does he travel alone? Why or why not?

2nd. para.

Does he like *the beaches*?
the night life?
the food?

_____ ?

Does he like the people? Why or why not?

During the day does he *swim at the beach*?
get a suntan?
relax by the swimming pool?
play golf?

_____ ?

In the evening does he *dance in a discotheque*?
gamble in a casino?
have a quiet dinner with a friend?

_____ ?

3rd para.

Does Donald spend a lot of money on his vacation?

At the end of his vacation does he want to return home? Why or why not?

THE TEACHER

ACTIVITY   With your partner, talk about your teacher. Using the choices you are given, you and your partner decide what you want to write. Then write four paragraphs. Each of you write on your own paper.

1st para.

When your teacher comes to class, does he/she *say "hello" to everyone*?
put his/her books on the desk?
take off his/her coat?
_____ ?

Does he/she tell the students *to get ready for class*?
to hand in the homework?
to stop talking?
to _____ ?

Does he/she take attendance?

2nd. para.

When the class is ready to begin, does the teacher explain what you are going to do during the class?

Then does he/she usually *teach a lesson at the blackboard*?
give you an activity to do?
give you an assignment in your book?
_____ ?

Does he/she answer your questions while you are working in class?

3rd para.

Is the class *easy*?
hard?   } Why?
just right?

Do the students pay attention to the teacher? Why or why not?

Do the students usually *work together as a whole class*?
work together in small groups?
_____ ?

4th para.

Is your teacher *a funny person*?
a serious person?
a happy person?
a friendly person?
a _____ ?

Are you happy that you are a student in his/her class? Why or why not?

ANOTHER GOOD FRIEND

ACTIVITY   Tell your partner or your group about a good friend. Then write about your friend. Write one paragraph.

1.   What is your friend's name?

2.   Is your friend married or single?

3.   Does your friend have any children?

4.   Where does your friend live?

5.   Does your friend work? Where? What does your friend do?

6.   Does your friend go to school? Where? What is your friend's curriculum?

7.   On weekends, does your friend like to *go to dances*?
     go to parties?
     go out on dates?
     go out with the family?
     stay home and watch TV?

8.   Does your friend have a happy life? Why or why not?

9.   Why is he or she a good friend?

A HOLIDAY IN MY COUNTRY

ACTIVITY   With your partner or your group talk about a holiday in your country that is not a holiday in the United States. Then write about this holiday. Write three paragraphs.

1st para.

What is the name of the holiday?

On what day or days do the people of your country celebrate it?

Is it a religious holiday or a political holiday or some other kind of holiday?

In what year did the people of your country first celebrate this holiday?

2nd. para.

What do the people do on this holiday?

Do they have a parade?
Do they dance in the streets?
Do they wear special clothes?
Do they cook a lot of food for friends and neighbors?
Do they stay at home and pray?

3rd para.

Why is this holiday important for the people of your country?

MY PARENTS

ACTIVITY Ask your partner or someone in your group the following questions. Then your partner or someone in your group will ask you the questions.

1. Where was your mother born?
2. Where was your father born?
3. When were they born?
4. Did they go to school? Where?
5. How long did they go to school?
6. Did they have brothers and sisters?
7. Did they live with their parents or with some other relatives?

Now write a paragraph about your parents. First read the paragraph below. You may use it as a model if you want to.

My Parents

My mother was born in San Juan, Puerto Rico in 1934. My father was born in Ponce, but I don't know when. My mother went to elementary school and then to Colegio San Juan. She finished high school. My father went to school in Ponce until the eighth grade. He didn't finish school because he had to help take care of his family. My mother had two brothers and two sisters. She lived with her parents. My father had three sisters and one brother. He lived with his parents until he was 14 years old. Then his father died and he went to live with an uncle. He worked in his uncle's store to help support his family.

MORE ABOUT ME

ACTIVITY Ask your partner or someone in your group the following questions. Then your partner or someone in your group will ask you the questions.

1. Where were you born?
2. When were you born?
3. What did your father do?
4. What did your mother do?
5. Did you go to elementary school? Where?
6. Did you like school? Why or why not?
7. Did you go to high school? Why or why not?
8. When did you come to the United States?
9. Do you miss your country? Why or why not?
10. Are you happy to be in the United States? Why or why not?

Now write a paragraph about yourself. First read the paragraph below. You may use it as a model if you want to.

More About Me

I was born in Cambodia in 1960. I grew up in a small village. My father was a farmer. My mother took care of me and my brothers and sisters. I went to elementary school in my village. I made many friends. I didn't go to high school because I had to help my father. When I was 19, I left Cambodia with my brother and came to the United States. Now we live in Portland, Oregon. I miss my country, but I am happy to be in the United States.

THE PARK

ACTIVITY Ask your partner or someone in your group these questions. Then your partner or someone in your group will ask you the questions.

1. Do you enjoy going to the park? Why or why not?

2. What is your favorite park? Why?

3. When did you last go there?

4. Who did you go with?

5. What did you do?

6. Did you have anything to eat or drink? What?

7. How long did you stay?

8. Did you have a good time?

THE PARK

ACTIVITY   Write a story about the park. Write one paragraph.

Last *Sunday*   did you go to _____ Park?
    Saturday   (name of park)
    week

   _____

Did you go with *your family*?
             a friend?
             alone?

          _____?

Was it *a nice day*?
      a warm day?
      a cool day?
      a windy day?

    _____?

Did you *play ball*?
      go swimming in the pool?
      go rowing on the lake?
      relax on a blanket?
      jog around the lake?

    _____?

Did you bring food with you or did you buy food in the park?

Did you eat *hot dogs and hamburgers*?
      fried chicken?
      salad?
      sandwiches?

    _____?

Did you spend *the whole day in the park*?
      the whole afternoon in the park?
      three hours in the park?

    _____?

When you went home, did you feel *tired*?
             happy?
             sad?   } Why?
             relaxed?

        _____?

AN EVENING OUT

ACTIVITY Ask your partner or someone in your group these questions. Then your partner or someone in your group will ask you the questions.

1. Do you like to go out on dates? Why or why not?
    Did you like to go out on dates before you were married?

2. Did you go out on dates in your country?
    Did you have to have a chaperone?

3. When did you last go out with someone?

4. Who did you go out with?

5. Where did you go?

6. Did you have a good time? Why or why not?

7. Would you like to go out with this person again?
    Why or why not?

AN EVENING OUT

ACTIVITY   Write a story about a date. Write your story in one paragraph.

Last *night*   did you go out with your *friend*?
     Friday   *husband*?
     Saturday   *wife*?

_____   _____?

Before you went out, were you *nervous*?
                                excited?   } Why?
                                happy?
                                _____? }

Did you go *out to dinner*?
           to the movies?
           to a show?
           dancing?

           _____?

Were you *comfortable*   with _____? Why?
         uncomfortable   (name of person)

           _____

Did you enjoy *the dinner*?
              the movie?   }
              the show?   } Why or why not?
              dancing?
              _____?   }

Afterwards, did you *walk around for a while*?
                    get something to eat?
                    go to a bar for drinks?
                    go home together?

                    _____?

Do you plan to go out with _____ again? Why or why not?
                              (name of person)

THE PHONE CALL

ACTIVITY Ask your partner or someone in your group these questions. Then your partner or someone in your group will ask you the questions.

1. Do you like to receive phone calls? Why or why not?

2. If someone calls you and you don't want to talk to that person, what do you do?

3. When did you last receive a phone call from someone you didn't want to talk to?

4. Who called you?

5. What did he/she want?

6. What did you tell him/her?

7. After the phone call, how did you feel? Why?

THE PHONE CALL

ACTIVITY   Write a story about an unpleasant phone call that you received. Write one paragraph.

Last night	did your	*ex-husband*	call you?
Yesterday		*ex-wife*	
This morning		*ex-boyfriend*	
		ex-girlfriend	

_____

_____

Were you surprised to hear from him/her? Why?

Did he/she tell you that he/she wanted *to visit you?*
to invite you out?
to discuss a problem?
to borrow some money?

to _____ ?

Did you tell him/her that you *didn't want to see him/her?*
didn't want to go out with him/her?
didn't have time to talk?
didn't have any money?

didn't _____ ?

Did he/she get angry at you? Why or why not?

Did you tell him/her *not to call you anymore?*
not to bother you anymore?
to call you next week?

_____ ?

After the phone call, how did you feel? Why?

THE TEST

ACTIVITY Ask your partner or someone in your group these questions. Then your partner or someone in your group will ask you the questions.

1. When you have to take a test, how do you feel? Why?

2. When did you last take a test?

3. What kind of test was it?

4. Did you study or practice for it?

5. Did you pass it?

6. Did you like the test? Why or why not?

7. Did you speak to others who took the test? Did they like it? Why or why not?

8. How will you prepare for the next test?

THE TEST

ACTIVITY   Write about a test that you took recently. Write three paragraphs.

1st para.

Did you take a test *yesterday*?
last week?
two weeks ago?

_____?

Was it *an English test*?
a math test?
a driving test?

a _____?

Did you prepare for the test *for one hour*?
for three hours?

_____?

Did you feel *nervous before the test*?
confident before the test?

2nd. para.

Was the test *45 minutes long*?
one hour long?
two hours long?

_____?

Was it *easy*?
difficult?

Did you *pass the test*?
fail the test?

Did you get *an A on the test*?
a B on the test?
75% on the test?

_____?

Did most of the students *pass the test*?
fail the test?

After the test did most of the students say that they *liked the test*?
didn't like the test? } Why?

3rd para.

Now do you feel *happy*?
sad?
depressed?
_____? } Why?

How will you prepare for the next test?

THE FIRST DAY OF ENGLISH CLASS

ACTIVITY Ask your partner or someone in your group these questions. Then your partner or someone in your group will ask you the questions.

1. Why did you decide to take an English course?

2. How did you feel on the first day of class? Why?

3. Did anything unusual happen to you? What?

4. What did the teacher do to make you feel comfortable?

5. What did the teacher tell you to do?

6. Did you understand everything the teacher said? If not, why?

7. Did you meet any of your classmates the first day? Who?

8. At the end of the first class, how did you feel? Why?

THE FIRST DAY OF ENGLISH CLASS

ACTIVITY   Write about the first day of your English course. Write three paragraphs.

1st para.

Did you decide to take
an English course *because you want to study in the United States?*
because you want to have a good job?
because you need English for your present job?
because you plan to live in the United States?
because you like the English language?

because _____ ?

On the first day of class were you *excited?*
happy?
nervous?
afraid?
_____ ?
} **Why?**

2nd. para.

Did your teacher seem *friendly?*
helpful?
strict?
_____ ?

Did your teacher try to make you feel comfortable and secure in the class?
How? *by smiling at you?*
by welcoming you to the class?
by speaking slowly?
by explaining everything carefully?
by _____ ?

Did your teacher tell you *to fill out a questionnaire?*
to introduce yourself?
to buy books for the next class day?
to do a homework assignment?
to _____ ?

Did you understand everything the teacher said?
Why not? *because you were nervous?*
because you didn't understand very much English?
because the teacher spoke too fast?
because _____ ?

Did you meet any of your classmates the first day? Who?

3rd para.

At the end of your first class how did you feel?
Did you want to come back to the next class?
Did you want to drop the course?
Did you have a stronger desire to learn English?
} **Why?**

THE DOCTOR

ACTIVITY With your partner talk about Nancy and her daughter or son. Using the choices you are given, you and your partner decide what you want to write. Then write two paragraphs. Each of you write on your own paper.

1st para.

Did Nancy take her { daughter / son } to the *hospital*?
  clinic?
  doctor?
  dentist?
  _____?

Did her { daughter / son } have *a cold*?
  the flu?
  a cut on the leg?
  a toothache?
  _____?

Were there *many people* in the waiting room?
  only a few people
  _____?

Did Nancy have to wait *a long time*?
  an hour?
  only a few minutes?
  only a short time?
  _____?

2nd para.

Did the *doctor* / *dentist* examine her { *daughter*? / *son*? }
_____

Did her { daughter / son } cry? Why or why not?

Did the *doctor* / *dentist* { *prescribe some medicine*?
  give her/him an injection?
  put a bandage on the cut?
  fill a cavity? }
_____

Did the *doctor* / *dentist* tell Nancy *to get the medicine right away*?
  to come back in one week?
  to call the next day?
  to _____?
_____

The next day / *Two days later* did her { daughter / son } feel *better*?
  worse?
  the same?
_____
  _____?

A DECISION

ACTIVITY With your partner talk about Peter's decision to come to the United States. Using the choices you are given, you and your partner decide what you want to write. Then write three paragraphs. Each of you write on your own paper.

1st para.

Did Peter decide
to come to the United States *because he wanted to study?*
because he wanted to make money?
because life was too hard in his country?
_____ ?

Did Peter decide to come *after he finished high school?*
before he finished high school?
when he was _____ *years old?*
_____ ?

Did his parents feel *happy about his decision?*
sad about his decision? } Why?

2nd para.

What year did he arrive in the United States?

When he first arrived, did he live *in Chicago?*
in San Francisco?
in New York?
in _____ ?

Did he live *with relatives?*
with a friend?
by himself?
_____ ?

Did he *get a job?*
go to school? } Why?

Was he *happy?*
homesick?

3rd para.

Six months ago, did Peter *meet someone special?*
get sick?
lose his job?
graduate from college?
_____ ?

Did he decide *to get married?*
to go back to his native country?
to learn more English?
to find a job?
to _____ ? } Why?

27

MORE ABOUT MY PARENTS

ACTIVITY Think about what your parents were like when you were a child. Use the following questions as a guide and then add any information you would like to. Write two paragraphs.

1st para.

What is the first thing you remember about your mother?

What did your mother look like?

> Was she tall, medium, or short?
> How much did she weigh?
> What did she usually wear?
> What color were her eyes and hair?

What did your mother do for you when you were a child?

What were the most important things you learned from your mother?

2nd para.

What is the first thing you remember about your father?

What did your father look like?

> Was he tall, medium, or short?
> How much did he weigh?
> What did he usually wear?
> What color were his hair and eyes?

What did your father do for you when you were a child?

What were the most important things you learned from your father?

MY FAVORITE RELATIVE

ACTIVITY   Write about your favorite relative when you were a child. You may write about a sister, brother, aunt, uncle, cousin, grandmother, grandfather, etc., but *not* your mother or father. Write two paragraphs.

1st para.

Who was your favorite relative when you were a child?

Where did he/she live?

How often did you see him/her?

What did you do together when you were a child?

Why was he/she your favorite relative?

How much did you love him/her?

What did you like most about this relative?

2nd para.

Where is your relative now?

Is he/she still your favorite?

Do you still have the same kind of relationship with him/her? Why or why not?

AN IMPORTANT PERSON

ACTIVITY Think about a person who is important to you. Who is this person? Why is this person important to you? Write two paragraphs.

1st para.

Who?

What is the name of the person who is important to you?
Is this person a relative, friend, neighbor, teacher, counselor?
How long have you known this person: all you life, only a short time, many years?
Where does this person live?
What does this person do?
Is there anything else you want to tell about this person?

2nd para.

Why is this person important to you?

Write about some, or all of the following:

What did this person do for you?
How did this person help to change your life?
What did you learn from this person?
What did you do for this person?
What do you want to do for this person?
How do you feel about this person?
How does this person feel about you?
What do you hope for the future?
Is there anything else you want to write about?

HAPPY BIRTHDAY

ACTIVITY Write about your birthday. Use the questions below as a guide. Write four paragraphs.

1st para.
Do you like birthdays? Why or why not?

How do you usually celebrate your birthday?

2nd para.
What did you do on your last birthday?

Did you have a party?
Did you have a special dinner?
Did you celebrate with relatives and friends?
Did you get any presents?

3rd para.
How will you celebrate your next birthday?

Is there anything that you didn't do last time that you *would like* to do next time?

4th para.
In general, are birthdays important? Why?

CHRISTMAS VACATION

ACTIVITY   Tell your partner or your group about how you celebrated Christmas when you were a child and how you plan to celebrate Christmas this year. After you have shared this information, write about your Christmas. You may use the following questions as a guide. Write five paragraphs.

1st para.

How did you celebrate Christmas when you were a child?

Did you have a party?
Did you go to church?
Did you have special meals?
Did you give presents?
Did you send greeting cards?
Did you decorate your home?

2nd para.

How will you celebrate Christmas this year?

Will you give a party?
Will you go to church?
Will you make a special meal?
Will you give gifts?
Will you send Christmas cards?
Will you decorate your home?
Will you have a Christmas tree?

3rd para.

Mention three things that you *won't* do.

4th para.

How will your Christmas this year be different from the way you celebrated it as a child?

5th para.

Did you enjoy Christmas more in your native country, or do you enjoy it more now? Why?

EASTER VACATION

ACTIVITY   Tell your partner or your group about how you celebrated Easter when you were a child and what you plan to do during the Easter vacation this year. After you have shared this information, write about your Easter. You may use the following questions as a guide. Write five paragraphs.

1st para.
How did you celebrate Easter when you were a child?

Did you go away or stay home?
Did you have any special dishes?
Did you go to church?
Did you get new clothes?

2nd para.
How will you celebrate Easter this year?

Will you go away or stay home?
Will you have any special meals?
Will you do anything special for the children in your family?
Will you buy any new clothes?
Will you clean your home?
Will you study?

3rd para.   Mention three things that you *won't* do this year that you *usually do* or *used to do.*

4th para.   How will your Easter this year be different from the way you celebrated it as a child?

5th para.   Did you enjoy Easter more in your native country, or do you enjoy it more now? Why?

A RELIGIOUS HOLIDAY

ACTIVITY   Which religious holiday is the most important to you? Tell your partner or your group about how you celebrated that holiday when you were a child and how you celebrated (or will celebrate it) this year. After you have shared this information, write about your holiday. You may use the following questions as a guide. Write five paragraphs.

1st para.

How did you celebrate the holiday when you were a child?

Did you have a party?
Did you go to religious services?
Did you have special meals?
What other customs or rituals did you follow?

2nd para.

How did you (will you) celebrate the holiday this year?

Did you (Will you) give a party?
Did you (Will you) go to religious services?
Did you (Will you) make a special meal?
What other customs or rituals did you (will you) follow?

3rd para.   Mention three things you didn't (won't) do.

4th para.   How was the holiday (How will the holiday be) different this year from the way you celebrated it as a child?

5th para.   Did you enjoy the holiday more in your native country, or do you enjoy it more now? Why?

A LETTER

ACTIVITY Write a letter to a friend or relative. The following questions can help you.

1. What are you doing right now?
2. What is the weather like?
3. Where are you going to school? What are you studying?
4. What else are you doing now?
5. What are you planning to do in the future?
   What courses are you planning to take?
   Where are you going during your next vacation?
6. What is your correspondent doing now? What are his/her plans?

Read the letter below. You may use it as a model if you want to.

888 Beach Avenue,
Miami, Florida
October 15, 19

Dear Ricardo,

I am sitting on a bench in my neighborhood park and enjoying the beautiful fall weather here. The wind is blowing and some leaves are falling. I am going to college now and I am studying English. I am also working part-time as an elevator operator.

I am now sharing an apartment with my brother Tony and his wife Sara. He is working in a factory and she is going to school. Together we are fixing up the apartment. Tony and Sara are planning to go back home for a visit at Christmas, but I am staying in the city to work.

Are you still going to school? What are you going to do at Christmas? Write to me soon.

Your friend,
Nelson

INTERACTING

COMPATIBILITY QUOTIENT

In what ways are you and your partner alike? In what ways are you different? You can find out by asking each other questions and comparing your answers.

ACTIVITY   *Step 1.* You and your partner make questions by filling in the blank spaces in questions 1–15. For numbers 9, 10, 14, and 15, make your own questions about things that are most important to you. You and your partner must write the same questions.

Step 2. When you have finished filling in the 15 questions, ask your partner the questions and write his/her answers on the answer sheet in complete sentences. Look at the example in the box below and on the answer sheet. Your partner will ask you the same questions. When *you* answer the questions, write only YES or NO on the answer sheet.

Step 3. When you have finished, turn to page 40 and do questions 16–40. Follow the same directions. After you have finished all of the questions and answers, turn back to page 39 to find your Compatibility Quotient.

> **Example**   Do you like to dance?

QUESTIONS

1. Are you married?

2. _____ _____ a citizen?

3. _____ _____ ___ happy person?

4. _____ nice clothes important to you?

5. Is your family important to you?

6. _____ religion important to you?

7. _____ money more important than anything else?

8. _____ love more important than anything else?

9. _____ ?

10. _____ ?

11. Would you like to have children? (If you don't have any)

12. _____ _____ _____ _____ be famous?

13. _____ _____ _____ _____ go back to live in your native country?

14. _____ ?

15. _____ ?

COMPATIBILITY QUOTIENT—ANSWER SHEET

Example	Your Answers	Your Partner's Answers
	YES or NO	Yes, she (he) likes to dance. or No, he (she) doesn't like to dance.

Your Answers　　　　　　　　　　　Your Partner's Answers

1. _____

2. _____

3. _____

4. _____

5. _____

6. _____

7. _____

8. _____

9. _____

10. _____

11. _____

12. _____

13. _____

14. _____

15. _____

Continue with questions and answers on next page.

Finding your compatibility quotient　　Add up the number of questions you both answered in the same way and divide that number by the total number of questions asked. For example, if you had the same answers to 30 questions out of 40, divide 30 by 40 (30 ÷ 40). Your answer: .75 or 75% compatibility.

To find compatibility quotient

A.　Write the total number of questions answered by both partners. _____

B.　Write the total number of questions answered the same way. _____

C.　Divide B by A.

16. Do you like to go to movies?

17. _____ _____ _____ _____ _____ _____ shows?

18. _____ _____ _____ _____ _____ _____ museums?

19. _____ _____ _____ _____ swim?

20. _____ _____ _____ _____ play tennis?

21. _____ _____ _____ _____ gamble?

22. _____ _____ _____ _____ listen to music?

23. _____ _____ _____ _____ eat in restaurants?

24. _____ _____ _____ _____ watch television?

25. _____ ?

26. _____ ?

27. Do you like animals?

28. _____ _____ _____ sports events?

29. _____ _____ _____ Chinese food?

30. _____ _____ _____ liver?

31. _____ _____ _____ vegetables?

32. _____ _____ _____ ice cream?

33. _____ ?

34. _____ ?

35. Do you like skiing?

36. _____ _____ _____ reading?

37. _____ _____ _____ traveling?

38. _____ _____ _____ riding a bicycle?

39. _____ ?

40. _____ ?

	Your Answers	*Your Partner's Answers*
16.	_____	_____
17.	_____	_____
18.	_____	_____
19.	_____	_____
20.	_____	_____
21.	_____	_____
22.	_____	_____
23.	_____	_____
24.	_____	_____
25.	_____	_____
26.	_____	_____
27.	_____	_____
28.	_____	_____
29.	_____	_____
30.	_____	_____
31.	_____	_____
32.	_____	_____
33.	_____	_____
34.	_____	_____
35.	_____	_____
36.	_____	_____
37.	_____	_____
38.	_____	_____
39.	_____	_____
40.	_____	_____

To find Compatibility Quotient, turn back to page 39.

STUDENT INTERVIEW

ACTIVITY   Pretend you are a counselor interviewing a student. You have to fill out the "Student Interview form." Think of the questions you must ask in order to get the answers you need to complete the form. First write the questions on the lines below. Then select a partner and take turns interviewing each other and filling out the form.

1. _____ ?

2. _____ ?

3. _____ ?

4. _____ ?

5. _____ ?

6. _____ ?

7. _____ ?

8. _____ ?

9. _____ ?

10. _____ ?

11. _____ ?

12. _____ ?

13. _____ ?

14. _____ ?

15. _____ ?

16. _____ ?

17. _____ ?

18. _____ ?

19. _____ ?

STUDENT INTERVIEW FORM

1. _____ 2. _____ 3. _____
    Last Name   First Name   Middle Initial

4. _____ _____
    Address: Number, Street, State   Zip Code

5. (   ) _____
    (Area Code) Phone Number

6. _____ 7. _____
    Date of Birth   Place of Birth

8. Father — _____ 9. Mother — _____
                        Parents' Names

10. _____ 11. _____
     Date of Arrival in the U.S.   Number of Years Living in the State.

12. _____
     Reasons for coming to the U.S.

_____

13. _____
     Reasons for going to school.

_____

14. _____
     Reasons for choosing this school.

_____

15. _____ 16. _____
     Date entered this school   Curriculum (Major Subject)

17. _____
     Career Goals

_____

18. _____
     Languages Spoken

19. _____
     Hobbies, Interests, etc.

_____
Signature of Interviewer

TAKING MESSAGES

The Caller   Make a phone call. The person you want to speak to is not in. Leave a message that includes all the information. Also be sure to give your name and phone number and the time you can be reached.

The Message-Taker   The person that the caller wants to speak to is not in. You take the message. Be sure to get the caller's name, phone number, and the time he or she can be reached. Then, write down the message.

1. **Call your teacher**   You won't be in class today. You will be back tomorrow. You would like to have the homework assignment. Tell why you won't be in school.

2. **Call your classmate**   Give your classmate the homework assignment for tomorrow for one of your classes. He (She) can call you back if there are any questions.

3. **Call a friend**   Arrange to meet a friend for dinner. Give the name of the restaurant, address, phone number, and time of the reservation. Your friend can call you back if there is a problem.

4. **Call your lawyer**   You're at the 23rd Precinct Police Station at 106th Street and Amsterdam Avenue. You need your lawyer's help immediately. The precinct phone number is 799–8724. The lawyer should ask for Sergeant Collins.

5. **Call your landlord**   Something in your apartment must be repaired immediately. Tell specifically what the problem is. Give your address and apartment number. You want to know when someone will come to fix it.

6. **Call your auto mechanic**   You want to know when your car will be ready, what the problem was, and how much it will cost.

7. **Call your boss**   You can't come to work today. Tell why. You could come in early tomorrow if your boss wants you to. You would like your boss to let you know.

8. **Call a store**   You are waiting for a delivery that hasn't arrived. Tell specifically what you ordered and when it was supposed to be delivered. Ask them to call you back to let you know when the order will be delivered.

9. **Call your babysitter**   You want your babysitter to take care of your child next Saturday night. Tell the time and for how many hours. The babysitter should call you back to let you know if he or she is available.

10. **Call the President**   You know how to solve the country's most difficult problem. The President should call you back right away because you are going out to a movie.

TAKING MORE MESSAGES

The Caller   Make a phone call. The person you want to speak to is not in. Leave a message that includes all the information. Also be sure to give your name and phone number and the time you can be reached.

The Message-Taker   The person that the caller wants to speak to is not in. You take the message. Be sure to get the caller's name, phone number, and the time he or she can be reached. Then, write down the message.

1. **Call your doctor**   Your six-year-old daughter has an earache and she is crying in pain. She has no fever. You gave her four children's aspirin one hour ago.

2. **Doctor calls**   Bring the sick child into the office at 3 P.M. Keep the child home from school today. If you can't bring the child in at 3 o'clock, call back.

3. **Call a friend**   Invite your friend to a party. Give the time, place, and reason for the party. Tell what to wear and what to bring. R.S.V.P. (You want your friend to call back to tell you if he or she can come.)

4. **Call a friend**   Your friend is coming to your party later. You want him or her to bring something to eat or drink to the party. You want your friend to call back to let you know if he or she will bring the food.

5. **Call a friend**   He or she left something at your house the day before. You want to know if your friend wants you to bring it into class next week or if he or she wants to come to your home to get it.

6. **Call the payroll office**   You didn't get this month's check. What happened? What should you do? It's urgent. Your bills are due.

7. **Call your neighbor**   You want to borrow her cat because there's a mouse in your apartment. Please hurry.

8. **Call a friend**   The father of your friend John died yesterday. The funeral will take place at the Broadway Funeral Home the day after tomorrow at 10 A.M. Your friend should call you if he/she wants a ride.

9. **Call a relative**   You (the father) just had a baby girl. Weight: 6 pounds, 8 ounces. Mother and daughter are fine. They are at St. Michael's Hospital. Phone: 477–0833.

10. **Call your boss**   You just won $3,000,000 in the lottery. You quit. She should send your last paycheck to you care of the Caribe Hilton in San Juan, Puerto Rico.

HOW TO

ACTIVITY

1. Think of a special skill that you have—something that you can do that most of the other students in the class probably do not know how to do. For example:

   Prepare a Special Dish
   Diaper a Baby
   Put Up Wallpaper
   Convert from Metric to English Measure
   Score in Bowling
   Play Checkers or Dominoes
   Repair a Broken Window
   Fasten a Tie

2. Select a partner. Choose a skill that your partner does not know. Explain it to him/her. Answer his/her questions.

3. Reverse roles. As the learner, you should ask questions and take notes. Be sure you understand the directions.

4. Write down the directions to the skill you are teaching. Give it a title: "How to . . ."

5. Write down the directions to the skill you have just learned about. Give it a title: "How to . . ."

6. Compare papers with your partner. Help each other make corrections.

FILLING IN

FIRE FIGHTERS

ACTIVITY   Read the following story. Then working as a group, choose two different words or short phrases for the blank spaces in each sentence. Any choice is correct if it makes sense in the story.

There are ten firemen in this (1) _picture_____ . They are fighting with each other

(2) _drawing_____ .

instead of (1) _____ the fire. Two men are (1) _____

(2) _____   (2) _____

the (1) _____ . One is telling the other how it (1) _____ .

(2) _____ .   (2) _____ .

This is what he is saying:

"This house is (1) _____ between two different fire companies. These

(2) _____

companies don't like each other. They are (1) _____ competitive. For example,

(2) _____

they have an annual (1) _____ contest and always end up fighting. They compete

(2) _____

in bowling and (1) _____ each other instead of the pins. They both

(2) _____

(1) _____ to fight the same fire at the same time, and of course they are fighting

(2) _____

each other instead. I'm (1) _____ that it's not my house.

(2) _____

DIRECTIONS Working by yourself, choose the word or short phrase in each sentence that you like best. Underline your choice. Then recopy the story with the words and phrases that you underlined.

Example

There are ten firemen in this (1) _picture_____ .

(2) _drawing_____ .

Recopy: _There are ten firemen in this picture. They are fighting with each_
other instead of . . .

49

MONEYBAGS

ACTIVITY Read the following story. Then working as a group, choose two different words or short phrases for the blank spaces in each sentence. Any choice is correct if it makes sense in the story.

Mr. P. J. Gorman, the man (1) _on the left_ , is a very (1) _rich_

(2) _with the cigar_ , (2) _wealthy_

man. You can tell by looking at him. He (1) _____ expensive cigars and drinks

(2) _____

imported (1) _____ . He (1) _____ a big house and he wears

(2) _____ . (2) _____

(1) _____ clothing. He does one very (1) _____ thing,

(2) _____ (2) _____

however. He (1) _____ his money at home in big (1) _____ .

(2) _____ (2) _____ .

He likes to sit (1) _____ his money.

(2) _____

His friend, Rocky Nelson, an ex- (1) _____ champion, is visiting him. Rocky

(2) _____

is the owner of a (1) _____ . Rocky (1) _____ the money. He

(2) _____ .   (2) _____

says something to (1) _____ about the money. What does he say?

(2) _____

DIRECTION A Working by yourself, choose the word or short phrase in each sentence that you like best. Underline your choice. Then recopy the story with the words and phrases that you underlined.

Example

Mr. P. J. Gorman, the man (1) __on the left__ , is a very

(2) __with the cigar__ ,

(1) __rich__ man.

(2) __wealthy__

Recopy: __Mr. P.J. Gorman, the man on the left, is a very wealthy man. You can__ __tell by looking at him. He ...__

DIRECTION B Write down the words that Rocky is saying to P. J. Then write what P. J. says to Rocky.

THE TIME MACHINE

ACTIVITY   Read the following story. Then working as a group, choose three different words or short phrases for the blank spaces in each sentence. Any choice is correct if it makes sense in the story.

"Crazy Doc" Johnson, head of the (1) _____ department at your school, says

(2) _____

(3) _____

he has invented a time machine that can (1) _____ people back in time. He wants

(2) _____

(3) _____

someone to test the machine and is offering (1) _____ to anyone who will try it.

(2) _____

(3) _____

You volunteer. Why? First of all, you want what he is offering. Secondly, "Crazy Doc" hasn't

(1) _____ anything yet that really worked. So you (1) _____

(2) _____   (2) _____

(3) _____   (3) _____

that you have nothing to lose.

Doc Johnson (1) _____ you into his strange-looking machine and asks you

(2) _____

(3) _____

when and where back into time you would like to (1) _____ . You tell him, and

(2) _____ .

(3) _____ .

you laugh to yourself because you know it won't (1) _____ .

(2) _____ .

(3) _____ .

Doc (1) _____ a (1) _____ and the machine starts

(2) _____ (2) _____

(3) _____ (3) _____

shaking. You (1) _____ your eyes. When the machine stops, you look around.

(2) _____

(3) _____

It has worked! You are back in the time and place that you asked for.

DIRECTION A   Working by yourself, choose the word or short phrase in each sentence that you like best. Underline your choice. Then recopy the story with the words and phrases that you underlined.

DIRECTION B   Write the conclusion of the story. Where does the machine take you? What year is it? Tell whom you meet and what you do.

CAUGHT IN THE ACT

ACTIVITY   Read the following story. Then working as a group, choose four different words or short phrases for the blank spaces in each sentence. Any choice is correct if it makes sense in the story.

We entered and sat at a table near the (1) _____ . The orchestra was just

                                 (2) _____ .

                                 (3) _____ .

                                 (4) _____ .

(1) _____ to warm up. It was a/an (1) _____ evening and the

(2) _____   (2) _____

(3) _____   (3) _____

(4) _____   (4) _____

club was filled with (1) _____ who wanted to dance. They were waiting impatiently

                   (2) _____

                   (3) _____

                   (4) _____

for the (1) _____ to begin. Finally the orchestra started to play. Their first number

    (2) _____

    (3) _____

    (4) _____

was (a) (1) _____ . My lover and I (1) _____ and walked to

    (2) _____ .   (2) _____

    (3) _____ .   (3) _____

    (4) _____ .   (4) _____

the dance floor. The music was (1) _____ . We danced the whole set without

             (2) _____ .

             (3) _____ .

             (4) _____ .

(1) _____ . When the orchestra took a break, my lover went (1) _____ .

(2) _____ .   (2) _____ .

(3) _____ .   (3) _____ .

(4) _____ .   (4) _____ .

When { he
       she } returned to our table, { she
                                      he } found me (1) _____ another

(2) _____

(3) _____

(4) _____

{ woman.
  man. }

DIRECTION A Working by yourself, choose the word or short phrase in each sentence that you like best. Underline your choice. Then recopy the story with the words and phrases that you underlined.

DIRECTION B Working as a group, discuss different possible endings for the story. Then by yourself, choose the ending that you like best and write your ending to the story.

GIFT BASKET

ACTIVITY   Look at the picture and then read the story below. Two parts of the story are missing: what the note said and what Charley said. Discuss the story with your partner or your group. Then by yourself fill in the missing parts of the story.

     Charley Moody was getting ready to go to bed. He was in his pajamas and was wearing his bathrobe. He was watching the 11 o'clock news. He head the doorbell ring. When he opened the door, no one was there except a baby lying in a basket on the front step. There was a note pinned to the baby. The note said:

"_____

_____

_____

_____."

    Charley read the note and then shouted, "_____

_____

_____

_____."

DIRECTIONS   Working by yourself, write the conclusion of the story.

A BAD DREAM

ACTIVITY   Look at the picture and then read the story below. Parts of the story are missing. Discuss the story with your partner or your group. Then by yourself, fill in the missing parts of the story.

Frank is 45 years old. He is 5 feet, 6 inches tall and weighs about 190 pounds. He lives in a big city with his wife and two children.

Frank has an interesting job. He _____

_____

_____

Usually Frank stands with his cart _____

_____

_____

_____

One summer night Frank had no business at all. No one wanted to buy his sausages. He became so frustrated that he ate four of his own sausages with lots of mustard and onions. Then he went home and went directly to bed.

That night, Frank had a bad dream. He dreamt _____

_____

_____

_____

_____

_____

_____

_____

_____.

Frank woke up in a sweat, which was strange because the air conditioner was on. His stomach was upset and he had a headache. He took an Alka Seltzer and went back to bed.

In the future, Frank will not _____

_____.

TALKING IT OVER

THE CHECKOUT LINE

Mr. Becker is standing in the checkout line at a supermarket with a basketful of groceries. It is the end of the day. He is tired. He wants to get home as quickly as possible. He is next in line to be checked out. He doesn't want anyone to get in front of him.

Mrs. Dorsey came into the supermarket to buy milk and cookies for her child. She is in a hurry. There is a long line. She asks Mr. Becker if she can go ahead of him.

ACTIVITIES   *Role-playing.* You and your partner decide who will be Mr. Becker and who will be Mrs. Dorsey. Say to each other the things that you think Mr. Becker and Mrs. Dorsey said to each other in the checkout line.

Dialogue writing. When you and your partner finish the conversation, write it down. Each of you write it on your own paper. Each of you write everything. Write the dialogue like this:

MRS. DORSEY: Excuse me, sir. May I get ahead of you?

MR. BECKER: I'm sorry.

MRS. DORSEY: _____

MR. BECKER: _____

Dialogue correcting. When you and your partner finish writing, check each other's papers and correct the mistakes you find. Then read your dialogue out loud two times. One time you will be Mrs. Dorsey and the other time you will be Mr. Becker. Listen for mistakes and correct them on your papers.

A CONVERSATION IN THE PARK

Carole is a young woman. She has two children but is divorced. She would like to meet someone and perhaps get married again. Yesterday Carole brought her children to the park. It was a beautiful spring day. Carole felt happy. She sat on a bench and watched her children play.

Richard is forty-seven years old. He lives alone. His wife died four years ago. His three children are married. He would like to meet a nice woman and perhaps get married again. Yesterday he went to the park during his lunch hour. He saw Carole sitting on a bench. He sat down next to her and began talking to her.

ACTIVITIES   *Role-playing.* You and your partner decide who will be Carole and who will be Richard. Say to each other the things you think Carole and Richard said to each other yesterday in the park.

Dialogue writing. When you and your partner finish the conversation, write it down. Each of you write it on your own paper. Each of you write everything. Write the dialogue like this:

RICHARD: Hi. It's a beautiful day.

CAROLE: Yes. It's a nice day to be in the park.

RICHARD: _____ .

CAROLE: _____ .

Dialogue correcting. When you and your partner finish writing, check each other's papers and correct the mistakes you find. Then read your dialogue out loud two times. One time you will be Carole and the other time you will be Richard. Listen for mistakes and correct them on your papers.

I WON'T PAY THE RENT

Tenant   There is no heat or hot water in your apartment. The toilet in your bathroom is not working properly. The super (janitor) doesn't clean the building or do anything else he is supposed to do. He sits on the front steps drinking and talking to his friends. The building is full of roaches, the halls are dirty, and you are angry. You complain to the landlord. You tell him you won't pay the rent until everything is fixed and he gets a new janitor (super) for the building.

Landlord   This building has an old boiler and it is broken. You called the repair service and they say it will take another week to fix it. You would like to get a new super (janitor), but they're hard to find. If the building is dirty and has roaches, it's because of the dirty tenants. You're not making enough profit on the building to maintain it properly. You want your rent right now.

ACTIVITIES   *Role-playing.* You and your partner decide who will be the tenant and who will be the landlord. Say to each other the things you think the tenant and the landlord would say to each other.

Dialogue writing. When you and your partner finish the conversation, write it down. Each of you write it on your own paper. Each of you write everything. Write the dialogue like this:

TENANT: _____

LANDLORD: _____

Dialogue correcting. When you and your partner finish writing, check each other's papers and correct the mistakes that you find. Then read your dialogue out loud two times. One time you will be the tenant and the other time you will be the landlord. Listen for mistakes and correct them on your papers.

HOME FOR THE HOLIDAY?

Jenny has lived in Boston for three years. Her parents still live in their native country. They want Jenny to come home for the holiday vacation.

Their reasons
{
She is their oldest child and they haven't seen her in two years.
Their other children are not at home.
They don't want to celebrate the holiday alone.
Jenny's mother is not feeling well.
}

Jenny does not want to go home for the holiday.

Her reasons
{
Her friends invited her to spend part of the holiday vacation with them.
She has a boyfriend and she wants to be with him.
She is going to school and she has a lot of work to do during the vacation.
It costs a lot of money to fly home and back.
Jenny is afraid her parents will ask her to stay with them and not return to Boston.
}

A week before the holiday, Jenny calls her parents on the phone to discuss the situation with them.

ACTIVITIES   *Role-playing.* You and your partner decide who will be Jenny and who will be the mother (or father). Say to each other the things you think Jenny and her mother (or father) said to each other when she called on the phone.

Dialogue writing. When you and your partner finish the conversation, write it down. Each of you write it on your own paper. Each of you write everything. Write the dialogue like this:

JENNY: _____

MOTHER (or FATHER): _____

Dialogue correcting. When you and your partner finish writing, check each other's papers and correct the mistakes that you find. Then read your dialogue out loud two times. One time you will be Jenny and the other time the mother (or father). Listen for mistakes and correct them on your papers.

FINAL GRADE

Student   Your English teacher gave you a final grade of C. You think you deserve a better grade. Your attendance was good. You passed all your tests and you did most of your homework. Besides, your friend got a higher grade and you know more English than him/her. You go to your teacher and ask for a better grade.

Teacher   You decide on final grades carefully. They are based on

1. the final examination (which includes a composition marked by other teachers).

2. all work done during the course.

3. how much progress the student made during the course.

This student did all the work and got a passing grade on the final exam, but didn't make much progress during the course. You do not want to raise the grade.

ACTIVITIES   *Role-playing.* You and your partner decide who will be the student and who will be the teacher. Say to each other the things you think the student and the teacher said to each other.

Dialogue writing. When you and your partner finish the conversation, write it down. Each of you write it on your own paper. Each of you write everything. Write the dialogue like this:

STUDENT: _____

TEACHER: _____

Dialogue correcting. When you and your partner finish writing, check each other's papers and correct the mistakes that you find. Then read your dialogue out loud two times. One time you will be the student and the other time you will be the teacher. Listen for mistakes and correct them on your papers.

TELLING STORIES

PICTURE STORY 1

ACTIVITY Discuss this picture with a partner. Together make up a story that explains what you see in the picture. Then write the story this way:

1. Explain what is happening right now in this picture. Describe the room. Tell where each person is and what he or she is doing. Tell how each person is reacting to the face in the window.

    Tell a story about these people. Who are they? Why is the man standing at the window? How does the story end? What will happen?

Write this story *by yourself*. Then correct it *together*. Write a title for the story.

PICTURE STORY 2

There are three people in this cartoon: Ed; Ed's wife, Mabel (she's the one smiling and talking); and her friend, Maryanne.

ACTIVITY Discuss this cartoon with a partner. Together, make up a story that explains what you see in the picture. Then write the story this way:

1. Explain what is happening *right now* in the picture.

2. Explain how this situation happen*ed* (Mabel is telling Maryanne how it happened).

3. Tell how the story ends. What *will* happen.

Write this story *yourself*. Then correct it *together*. Write a title for the story.

PICTURE STORY 3

ACTIVITY Talk about this photograph with your partner or your group. Together, make up a story that explains the photograph. Who are the two people? Where are they? Why are they smiling?

Then, write the story yourself.

After you have finished, correct it together with a partner.

Write a title for the story.

PICTURE STORY 4

ACTIVITY   Discuss this picture with your partner. Together, make up a story that explains the picture.

Then write this story *by yourself.* When you have finished, correct it with your partner. Write a title for the story.

PICTURE STORY 5

ACTIVITY Talk about this photograph with your partner or your group. Together, make up a story that explains the picture.

Then, write the story yourself.

Correct it together with a partner. Write a title for the story.

PICTURE STORY 6

ACTIVITY Pretend you are either the man or the woman and you are running in the park. Who is the other person? What do you see? How do you feel? Write your thoughts as quickly as you can.

Then share your writing with your partner, group, or instructor.

On another piece of paper, write a story about the photograph. Give it a title.

PUTTING AN END TO IT

ROBERT

Robert came to the United States with his parents and his younger sister when he was twelve. They lived in New York, and Robert went to school there. His father died when Robert was fourteen. After his father's death, Robert became much closer to his mother. He took care of her and protected her.

His mother remarried when he was sixteen. He tried very hard to like his stepfather, but his stepfather wouldn't accept him. Maybe he was jealous of the close relationship between Robert and his mother. The stepfather treated Robert very badly. Robert was in high school, and he didn't have any money. Day by day it was becoming more difficult for him to live in the same house with his stepfather. It was hard for Robert to talk to his mother about his feelings because he knew that she loved her new husband.

ACTIVITY This is the beginning of a story. How would you finish this story? Discuss this with your partner or group. Then finish the story *by yourself:*

What decision did Robert make?
How did Robert's mother react to his decision?
What, if anything, changed between Robert and his mother?
What, if anything, changed between Robert and his stepfather?

SURPRISE PACKAGE

It was Saturday, June 13, a beautiful sunny day. I remember it well because that day my life changed—and it will never be the same again.

Here's what happened. I was just finishing my breakfast when the doorbell rang. It was a messenger with a package for me. I signed for it, brought it inside, and put it down on the hall table. I didn't have any idea what it was, or who had sent it. It was very puzzling.

I quickly took off the wrapping paper, and underneath there was a box with a ribbon around it. I untied the ribbon and opened the box.

ACTIVITY   Discuss the story with your partner or your group. Then write the ending of the story yourself. Tell what you found in the box and how it changed your life.

THE NOTE IN THE BOTTLE

I was walking along the beach one evening with my friend John. There was a full moon and the rippling waves glittered white in the moonlight. Suddenly we saw an object bobbing up and down in the waves. It was a bottle, and we could see that there was something inside it.

I walked out into the water and grabbed the bottle just as a big wave came in. I stumbled out of the water soaking wet and laughing. "I hope there's something interesting in this bottle," I said. There was. Inside the bottle we found a note and an old gold coin.

We read the note. It said:

ACTIVITY   Discuss this story with your partner or your group. Then write the ending of the story by yourself. Write the exact words in the note and then tell what you and John did.

JULIA'S STORY

Julia was eighteen years old and she was finishing high school. She wanted to be a professional, but there were few opportunities in her country. First, it was difficult to go to school because it was expensive, and priority was given to men. Second, even if she could go to school, there were very few jobs available. Finally, her parents did not approve and would not help her.

Julia had an older brother who lived in New York. He said she could come to live with him and go to school at the same time. There were disadvantages to going to New York. She had a boyfriend, and he didn't want her to go. She knew that New York was dangerous and dirty and cold in the winter. She knew she would have to learn English and that it would be difficult for her.

Julia thought about going to New York, and she considered the advantages and disadvantages.

ACTIVITY   This is the beginning of a story. How would you finish this story? Discuss this with your partner or group. Then finish the story by yourself: What did Julia decide to do? Tell why. Also tell what happened to her.

If she decided to go to New York:
   How did she explain her decision to her parents and boyfriend?
   What happened to her after she came to New York?

If she decided to stay in her country:
   What did she do about her ambitions to get an education and become a professional? Did she have
       to give them up, or was she able to work out a plan?
   Was Julia happy or unhappy with her decision? Explain why.

KEEPING IT PERSONAL

A BIRTHDAY CARD

ACTIVITY   Write a birthday card for someone you love.

Happy Birthday
Joyeux Anniversaire
Feliz Cumpleaños

A CHRISTMAS CARD

ACTIVITY   Write a Christmas card for the best teacher you ever had. Tell him or her what you appreciate most.

Happy Holidays
Meilleurs Voeux
Felices Fiestas

A DAYDREAM

ACTIVITY Imagine that you are sitting in the tree or lying under it. You are alone; no one else is near you. There isn't any noise. The day is very beautiful.

Daydream for ten minutes. Then write some of your daydream.

A DEAR JOHN LETTER

Dear John,

   Last night I was thinking about you. You asked me on the telephone but I didn't answer because I wasn't sure what I wanted to say. But now I will tell you the truth: I don't love you anymore because I already have a nicer man than you. He is a professional and he pays for my classes.

   Anyway, I don't love you. Don't think this is because you have other women. No, I don't think it is that. You have always done that.

   Now I don't want anything from you. Please, don't bother me anymore.

Goodbye,
Liliana

ACTIVITY   Write a letter to someone you used to love but don't love anymore. Tell that person why you don't love him or her.

A LOVE LETTER

ACTIVITY   Write a letter to someone you love telling why you love him or her and how much you love him or her.

EXERCISING

MY BROTHER

ACTIVITY   Read the story below and fill in the blanks with the *simple present* form of the verb. Where you see _____ write the negative form of the verb.
(neg.)

My brother _____ school. He _____ very hard. He
              like   study

_____ to mind. He also _____ . My brother and I
    seem (neg.)   work

_____ a lot of time together. We _____ along very well. We
    spend   get

_____ .
    fight (neg.)

MY CLASSMATE

ACTIVITY   Read the story below and fill in the blanks with the *simple present* form of the verb. Where you see _____ write the negative form of the verb.
(neg.)

My classmate's name _____ Elizabeth. She _____ from
                          be   come

Greece. She _____ 22 years old. She _____ in Westwood
                be   live

with her mother, father, and three sisters. Elizabeth _____ married. She
                                                          be (neg.)

_____ any children, but she _____ to have a son and a
    have (neg.)   hope

daughter in the future. She is studying English because she _____ to be a bilingual
                                                                want

secretary. She also _____ that English _____ a beautiful
                        think   be

language. In her free time, Elizabeth _____ tennis, _____
                                          play   read

good books, and _____ out with her boyfriend. I _____ happy
                    go   be

that Elizabeth _____ my classmate.
                    be

93

MY DREAM HOUSE

ACTIVITY   Read the story below and fill in the blanks with the *simple present* form of the verb. Where you see _____ write the negative form of the verb.
(neg.)

I _____ in an apartment in a big city. The city _____
live   be

beautiful. I often _____ about having my own house in the country. When I
dream

_____ , I _____ a red house with many tall trees. There
dream   see

_____ any other houses near it. Inside the house there _____
be (neg.)   be

a big living room with a fireplace. On one side of the living room there _____ a big
be

window. From the window you can _____ a clear blue lake with a mountain behind
see

it. Next to the living room _____ a small kitchen and upstairs
be

_____ two bedrooms and a bathroom.
be

It _____ very hot during the summer. I _____ about the
be   think

cool water of the lake and the shade of the trees near my dream house. In winter, when it

_____ cold, I _____ that I _____ in my
be   imagine   be

living room in front of a warm fire in the fireplace. Outside the snow _____ and the
fall

wind _____ , but I _____ it. I _____
blow   mind (neg.)   be

nice and warm.

A MARRIED COUPLE

ACTIVITY   Read "A Married Couple." Below are *answers* about the story. On the lines at the left, write *questions* that go with the answers.

John and Carole are married. They love each other very much. They want to have children, but they don't have any yet. They both work. John is an auto mechanic and Carole is a dental technician. They make good salaries. They spend every evening together except Monday and Thursday. On Mondays Carole takes classes at the college and John stays home and watches Monday night football or reads a book. On Thursdays John goes out bowling with friends and Carole usually goes to a movie with a friend of hers. They think it's important to have some time away from each other.

	Questions	*Answers*
1.	_____ ?	Yes, they are.
2.	_____ ?	Yes, they do.
3.	_____ ?	No, not yet.
4.	_____ ?	Yes, they both work.
5.	_____ ?	He is an auto mechanic.
6.	_____ ?	She is a dental assistant.
7.	_____ ?	Yes, they do.
8.	_____ ?	On Mondays.
9.	_____ ?	They go out separately.
10.	_____ ?	Because they think it's important to have time away from each other.

ALLEN

ACTIVITY   Read "Allen." Below are *answers* about the story. On the lines at the left, write *questions* that go with the answers.

I have a good friend named Allen. He is forty years old. He is 5 feet, 8 inches tall and weighs about 150 pounds. He has short, dark brown hair and wears eyeglasses. He's an attractive-looking man.

Allen comes from Connecticut and lives in New York City now. He used to live in Connecticut with his wife and two children, but he is divorced and his two children are going to college. Now Allen lives alone in his own apartment in Manhattan.

Allen has four sisters and one brother. They are all married and live near New York. His mother is dead and his father is in a nursing home.

Allen is a lawyer. He likes his work and makes a lot of money. He is a very generous and happy person.

	Questions		*Answers*
1.	_____	?	Forty.
2.	_____	?	5'8".
3.	_____	?	150 pounds.
4.	_____	?	Dark brown.
5.	_____	?	Connecticut.
6.	_____	?	No, he is divorced.
7.	_____	?	Yes, he has two children.
8.	_____	?	He is a lawyer.
9.	_____	?	Yes, he does.
10.	_____	?	Yes, he is.

MONEYBAGS

ACTIVITY Look at the story and picture, "Moneybags," on pages 50 and 51. Below are *answers* about the story. On the lines at the left, write *questions* that go with the answers.

Questions	Answers
1. _____ ?	P. J. Gorman and Rocky Nelson.
2. _____ ?	A cigar.
3. _____ ?	Talking.
4. _____ ?	In big bags.
5. _____ ?	He doesn't trust banks.
6. _____ ?	Yes, he does.
7. _____ ?	No, he doesn't.
8. _____ ?	Yes, they are.
9. _____ ?	Yes, he is.
10. _____ ?	No, he isn't.

THE TIME MACHINE

ACTIVITY Look at the story on pages 52 and 53. Below are *answers* about the story. on the lines on the left, write *questions* that go with the answers.

Questions	Answers
1. _____ ?	"Crazy Doc."
2. _____ ?	A time machine.
3. _____ ?	You.
4. _____ ?	You have nothing to lose.
5. _____ ?	(a year) _____ .
6. _____ ?	(a place) _____ .
7. _____ ?	Yes, it does.
8. _____ ?	No, he isn't.
9. _____ ?	No, you don't.
10. _____ ?	Yes, you do.

ABOUT ME

ACTIVITY Read the story "About Me" on page 4. Below are *answers* about the story. Write a *question* that goes with each answer.

	Questions	*Answers*
1.	_____ ?	Tom.
2.	_____ ?	I come from Cambodia.
3.	_____ ?	I live at 193 Union Ave.
4.	_____ ?	I live with my brother.
5.	_____ ?	Yes, I have another brother and two sisters.
6.	_____ ?	They live in Cambodia.
7.	_____ ?	My major subject is Electrical Technology.
8.	_____ ?	I want to become an engineer.
9.	_____ ?	My hobbies are dancing and going to the movies.
10.	_____ ?	Yes, I do.

A GOOD FRIEND

ACTIVITY Read the story "A Good Friend" on page 5. Below are *answers* about the story. Write a *question* that goes with each answer.

	Questions	*Answers*
1.	_____ ?	Marie.
2.	_____ ?	Haitian.
3.	_____ ?	20.
4.	_____ ?	5'3".
5.	_____ ?	110 pounds.
6.	_____ ?	Brown.
7.	_____ ?	A skirt and a sweater.
8.	_____ ?	Yes, she does.
9.	_____ ?	Yes, she is.
10.	_____ ?	Sports, music, and children.

THE CLASS

ACTIVITY   Read the story below and fill in the blanks with the *simple present form* of the verb. Where you see _____(neg.) write the negative form of the verb.

John _____ in class. William _____. Freddy and
                  be   be (neg.)

Charlie _____ here, but they _____ to work. Sarah
                  be   want (neg.)

_____ like she _____ to go home. Allen
        look   want

_____ to do his homework. Sam _____ the work. Some
     like (neg.)   understand (neg.)

students _____ too much, but most of them _____ anything.
                  talk   say (neg.)

Harry _____ what to do. Barbara _____ all the time. Philip
          know (neg.)   cry

_____ to work, but Dulce _____ bothering him. It
        try   keep

_____ 12 o'clock. The class _____ over. Thank God!
        be   be

ACTIVITY   Below are *answers* about the story, "The Class." On the lines at the left, write *questions* that go with each answer.

Questions	*Answers*
1. _____ ?	John.
2. _____ ?	No, he isn't.
3. _____ ?	Yes, they are.
4. _____ ?	No, they don't.
5. _____ ?	No, he doesn't.
6. _____ ?	Talk too much.
7. _____ ?	Barbara.
8. _____ ?	Dulce keeps bothering him.
9. _____ ?	12 o'clock.
10. _____ ?	Yes, it is.

RICHARD'S PROBLEM

ACTIVITY   Read the story below and fill in the blanks with the *simple present tense* form of the verb. Where you see _____ write the negative form of the verb.

(neg.)

Richard _____ some advice. He _____ in a big city with

need   live

his wife and two children. He _____ to move to a better neighborhood, but he

want

_____ if he should move at this time. In the first place, he

know (neg.)

_____ in a store near his home. He _____ to his job every day.

work   walk

If he _____ , he will have to spend money traveling to work. Second, his two

move

children _____ the school they are attending now. They _____

like   have

many friends in school. Maybe they won't like to go to a different school in a different neighborhood. In

the third place, Richard _____ a very good salary at his job. He

make (neg.)

_____ enough to support his family now, but he _____ sure if

earn   be (neg.)

he can support his wife and children in a new apartment where the rent is a lot higher. Richard and his

wife often _____ about their situation. They _____ to move,

talk   prefer

but they can't decide because they _____ the problems they will have if they move.

realize

ACTIVITY   Below are *answers* about the story, "Richard's Problem." On the lines at the left write *questions* that go with each answer.

	Questions	*Answers*
1.	_____ ?	Some advice.
2.	_____ ?	In a big city.
3.	_____ ?	To move to a better neighborhood.
4.	_____ ?	In a store near his home.
5.	_____ ?	Enough to support his family.
6.	_____ ?	He walks.
7.	_____ ?	No, he doesn't.
8.	_____ ?	No, he isn't.
9.	_____ ?	No, he doesn't.
10.	_____ ?	Yes, they do.

CHARLIE'S GROCERY

ACTIVITY   Read the story below and fill in the blanks with the *simple present* form of the verb. Where you see _____ (neg.) write the negative form of the verb.

Charlie _____ own _____ a small grocery. He _____ be _____ a nice guy. All the people in the neighborhood _____ know _____ he _____ be _____ a nice guy. Charlie's store _____ have _____ a little of everything. It _____ carry _____ all kinds of groceries. For the kids there _____ be _____ snacks and sodas. In the back there _____ be _____ a shelf of school supplies. Behind the counter Charlie _____ keep _____ cigarettes. People _____ run _____ in and out all day long. Sometimes one person _____ come _____ in five or six times a day. Charlie _____ mind (neg.) _____ all the business. Charlie _____ open (neg.) _____ his store until 7 A.M. but most customers _____ come (neg.) _____ in before 7:30. The kids _____ start _____ arriving at 8 o'clock. When they _____ leave _____ for school it _____ be _____ quiet for a while. Then the women _____ begin _____ to come in. Some of them just _____ want _____ to talk. Others _____ buy _____ a few things and leave.

ACTIVITY   Below are *answers* about the story. Write *questions* that go with the answers.

	Questions		Answers
1.	_____	?	Charlie.
2.	_____	?	Yes, he is.
3.	_____	?	All the people.
4.	_____	?	A little of everything.
5.	_____	?	All kinds of groceries.
6.	_____	?	Yes, there are.
7.	_____	?	Yes, there is.
8.	_____	?	Cigarettes.
9.	_____	?	At 8 o'clock.
10.	_____	?	No, he doesn't.

JOSE'S NEW YORK

ACTIVITY Read the story below and fill in the blanks with the *simple present* form of the verb. Where you see _____ write the negative form of the verb.

(neg.)

Jose _____ New York. He frequently _____ up and

like   walk

down Broadway and _____ at the people. He often _____ to

look   stop

watch the things that _____ on. Vendors _____ fruits and

go   sell

vegetables. People _____ where they _____ and often

look (neg.)   walk

_____ into others. There _____ much concern for other

bump   be (neg.)

people. But there _____ good things too. Some people _____

be   stop

and _____ Hello. Someone may _____ on a little show. It

say   put

_____ what _____ . It _____ a lot of

matter (neg.)   happen   be

fun.

ACTIVITY Below are answers about the story, "Jose's New York." On the lines at the left, write questions that go with the answers.

Questions	*Answers*
1. _____ ?	New York.
2. _____ ?	Up and down Broadway.
3. _____ ?	Yes, he does.
4. _____ ?	No, they don't.
5. _____ ?	Hello.
6. _____ ?	A little show.
7. _____ ?	Fruits and vegetables.
8. _____ ?	No, it doesn't.
9. _____ ?	Yes, it is.
10. _____ ?	Jose.

SCHOOL DAYS

ACTIVITY   Read the story below and fill in the blanks with the *past tense* form of the verb. Where you see _____ write the negative form of the verb.
(neg.)

When I _____ young, I always _____ to attend school,
be   want

but I _____ old enough. I _____ my older sister go to school
be (neg.)   watch

every day and I _____ more and more jealous. Finally the day
get

_____ . I _____ early in the morning and
come   wake up

_____ my best dress. I _____ so excited I
put on   be

_____ to eat breakfast. Then my mother _____ me to school.
want (neg.)   take

A lot of strange children _____ there. They _____ to me. The
be   talk (neg.)

teacher _____ . I _____ asleep at my desk. When I
smile (neg.)   fall

_____ home I _____ . I _____ that I
return   cry   decide

_____ school.
like (neg.)

MY PARENTS

ACTIVITY   Read the story below and fill in the blanks with the *past tense* form of the verb. Where you see _____ write the negative form of the verb.
(neg.)

My mother _____ born in San Juan, Puerto Rico in 1934. My father
be

_____ born in Ponce, but I _____ when. My mother
be   know (neg.)

_____ to a public elementary school and then to Colegio San Juan. She
go

_____ high school. My father _____ to school in Ponce until
finish   go

the eighth grade. He _____ school because he _____ to help
finish (neg.)   have

take care of his mother. My mother _____ two brothers and two sisters. She
have

_____ with her parents. My father _____ any sisters or
live   have (neg.)

brothers. He _____ with his parents very long because his father
live (neg.)

_____ and his mother _____ sick. He
die   get

_____ with an uncle and _____ in his uncle's store so that he
stay   work

_____ help support his mother.
can

103

GIFT BASKET

ACTIVITY   Read the story below and fill in the blanks with the *past tense* form of the verbs. Where you see _____ (neg.) write the negative form of the verb.

Charley Moody _____ ready to go to bed. He _____ in
                        get   be

his pajamas and he _____ on his bathrobe. He _____ the 11
                          have   watch

o'clock news. Then he _____ the doorbell ring. When he _____
                            hear   open

the door he _____ what he _____ . He
                    like (neg.)   see

_____ a baby lying in a basket on his front step. There _____
        find   be

a note pinned to the baby. It _____ from the mother and _____
                                        be   tell

why she _____ take care of her baby. She _____ Mr. Moody
              can (neg.)   ask

to take care of the baby until she _____ do it herself. When he
                                              can

_____ the note, he _____ angry and
        read   get

_____ . He _____ the mother _____
        shout   hope   will

hear him. He _____ that she _____ irresponsible. He
                      say   be

_____ to give her money to care for her baby. But she _____
        offer   come (neg.)

back. Charley _____ to call the police, but he _____ at the
                      want   look

cute, smiling baby and _____ to care for it until the mother
                                decide

_____ .
        return

CAUGHT IN THE ACT

ACTIVITY   Read the story "Caught in the Act" on pages 54 and 55. Below are *answers* about the story. On the lines at the left write *questions* that go with each answer.

Questions	Answers
1. _____ ?	Near the dance floor.
2. _____ ?	Warming up.
3. _____ ?	A beautiful night.
4. _____ ?	Many young couples.
5. _____ ?	The orchestra to begin.
6. _____ ?	A Salsa.
7. _____ ?	Walked to the dance floor.
8. _____ ?	Danced the whole set.
9. _____ ?	To the telephone.
10. _____ ?	Another man/woman.

A DINNER GUEST

ACTIVITY   Read the story below and fill in the blanks with the *past tense* form of the verbs. Where you see _____ write the negative form of the verb.
(neg.)

Last night John and Mary _____ a friend to dinner. They
    invite

_____ roast leg of lamb. They _____ a good Spanish wine. It
    have   serve

_____ $5. Their guest _____ any because she
    cost   drink (neg.)

_____ on a diet. She _____ a potato but she
    be   eat

_____ any butter on it. The guest _____ some flowers. After
    put (neg.)   bring

dinner they _____ for a while. Then they _____ television.
               talk   watch

They _____ up late because they _____ too tired. They
        stay (neg.)   be

_____ their guest home at 10:30. It _____ cold and she
    send   be

_____ a cab home. Then John and Mary _____ to bed.
    take   go

ACTIVITY   Below are *answers* about the story, "A Dinner Guest." On the lines at the left, write *questions* that go with the answers.

	Questions	*Answers*
1.	_____ ?	Last night.
2.	_____ ?	Roast leg of lamb.
3.	_____ ?	$5.
4.	_____ ?	No, she didn't.
5.	_____ ?	She was on a diet.
6.	_____ ?	Yes, she did.
7.	_____ ?	Some flowers.
8.	_____ ?	Yes, it was.
9.	_____ ?	No, they didn't.
10.	_____ ?	At 10:30.

MEXICO CITY

ACTIVITY   Read the story below and fill in the blanks with the *past tense* form of the verbs. Where you see _____ write the negative form of the verb.
(neg.)

John _____ Mexico City. He frequently _____ up and
        like   walk

down the avenues and _____ at all the things that people
                        look

_____ . He also _____ to what they said. Although he
        do   listen

_____ Spanish and he _____ everything, he
    speak (neg.)   understand (neg.)

_____ enough to get along. He often _____ to look in shop
        know   stop

windows. He _____ trouble buying things but it _____
                have   be (neg.)

difficult for him to order meals in restaurants. He _____ enough Spanish for that.
                                                        speak

The best thing of all _____ that he _____ sick. Everyone else
                        be   get (neg.)

_____ . He _____ that Mexican food
        do   decide

_____ with him.
    agree

ACTIVITY   Below are *answers* about the story, "Mexico City." On the lines at the left, write *questions* that go with the answers.

<table>
<tr><td align="center">*Questions*</td><td></td><td align="center">*Answers*</td></tr>
<tr><td>1. _____</td><td>?</td><td>Yes, he did.</td></tr>
<tr><td>2. _____</td><td>?</td><td>Up and down the avenues.</td></tr>
<tr><td>3. _____</td><td>?</td><td>The people.</td></tr>
<tr><td>4. _____</td><td>?</td><td>No, he didn't.</td></tr>
<tr><td>5. _____</td><td>?</td><td>To look in shop windows.</td></tr>
<tr><td>6. _____</td><td>?</td><td>John.</td></tr>
<tr><td>7. _____</td><td>?</td><td>Buying things.</td></tr>
<tr><td>8. _____</td><td>?</td><td>No, it wasn't.</td></tr>
<tr><td>9. _____</td><td>?</td><td>Everyone else.</td></tr>
<tr><td>10. _____</td><td>?</td><td>That Mexican food agreed with him.</td></tr>
</table>

FONG CHI'S EXPERIENCE

ACTIVITY   Read the story below and fill in the blanks with the *past tense* form of each verb. Where you see _____ write the negative form of the verb.
(neg.)

Fong Chi _____ born in Hong Kong. He _____ to come
                        be   decide

to San Francisco four years ago to find a better life. When he _____ at the airport,
                                                                      arrive

he _____ any money. He _____ to live with his uncle.
        have (neg.)   go

His uncle _____ rich. He _____ Fong Chi that he
                be (neg.)   tell

_____ to look for a job. Fong Chi _____ hard to find a job, but
        have   try

it _____ very difficult because he _____ English. Finally he
        be   speak (neg.)

_____ a job in a factory in Chinatown. There _____ many
        find   be

other workers in the factory besides Fong Chi. None of them _____ English, either.
                                                                  speak

After a few weeks, Fong Chi _____ the factory. He _____ all
                                  leave   like (neg.)

the hard work and the low pay. His uncle and his other relatives _____ happy about
                                                                      be (neg.)

that. They _____ the money that he _____ to help pay the
                need   earn

household expenses. Fong Chi _____ the situation. Soon he
                                  realize

_____ another job.
        find

ACTIVITY Below are *answers* about the story, "Fong Chi's Experience." On the lines at the left, write *questions* that go with the answers.

Questions	*Answers*
1. _____?	In Hong Kong.
2. _____?	To find a better life.
3. _____?	Four years ago.
4. _____?	No, he didn't.
5. _____?	His uncle.
6. _____?	No, he wasn't.
7. _____?	Because he didn't speak English.
8. _____?	He didn't like the hard work and the low pay.
9. _____?	No, they weren't.
10. _____?	Yes, he did.

MY UNCLE CARMINE

ACTIVITY Read the story below and fill in the blanks with the *past tense* form of each verb. Where you see _____ write the negative form of the verb.
(neg.)

My Uncle Carmine _____ to come to my house every weekend. He
use

_____ to hunt. He _____ in a big city and we
love   live

_____ a house in the country. Since he _____ hunt in the city,
have   can (neg.)

he _____ to visit us. He always _____ carrying two loaves of
come   arrive

Italian bread. I _____ that bread but I never _____ enough.
like   get

He _____ really my uncle but just an old friend of the family. But he
be (neg.)

_____ a very good friend. He _____ me hunting with him
be   take

every weekend. We _____ through the woods and _____
walk   hunt

rabbits. One weekend we _____ six. One winter I _____ out
shoot   go

without my jacket and _____ a cold. I _____ to stay in bed
catch   want (neg.)

but my parents _____ me. I _____ a terrible time. But usually
make   have

I _____ okay and when it _____ cold I _____.
be   be   mind (neg.)

When we _____ hungry we _____ and
feel   stop

_____ a fire. Uncle Carmine _____ sausage over the fire and
build   cook

we _____ it with big chunks of his bread. We _____ such a
eat   have

good time, we _____ to leave.
want (neg.)

ACTIVITY Read the story. Below are *answers* about the story, "My Uncle Carmine". On the lines at the left, write *questions* that go with the answers.

<table>
<tr><td align="center">*Questions*</td><td align="center">*Answers*</td></tr>
<tr><td>1. _____ ?</td><td>Every weekend.</td></tr>
<tr><td>2. _____ ?</td><td>Hunt.</td></tr>
<tr><td>3. _____ ?</td><td>Because he couldn't hunt in the city.</td></tr>
<tr><td>4. _____ ?</td><td>Italian bread.</td></tr>
<tr><td>5. _____ ?</td><td>No, he wasn't.</td></tr>
<tr><td>6. _____ ?</td><td>Yes, he was.</td></tr>
<tr><td>7. _____ ?</td><td>Rabbits.</td></tr>
<tr><td>8. _____ ?</td><td>Six.</td></tr>
<tr><td>9. _____ ?</td><td>Sausage and bread.</td></tr>
<tr><td>10. _____ ?</td><td>No, they didn't.</td></tr>
</table>

TOMORROW

ACTIVITY Read the story below and fill in the blanks with the *future tense* form of each verb. Where you see _____ (neg.) write the negative form of the verb.

Tomorrow morning I _____ to the city. I _____ for two
                        return   drive

hours. I _____ on the way. I _____ gas if I need it. I
           stop (neg.)   get

_____ home about noon. I _____ lunch and then I
   arrive   have

_____ some phone calls. I _____ time to relax. I
   make   have (neg.)

_____ down and _____ to write a report. I
   sit   start

_____ it by tomorrow night because it is due the next day. It
   finish

_____ about twenty pages long. When I am finished, I_____
   be   eat

dinner and _____ it easy. I _____ TV and I
              take   watch (neg.)

_____ out. I _____ just _____ down
   go (neg.)   lie

and _____ to sleep.
       go

GOING TO COLLEGE

ACTIVITY Read the story below and fill in the blanks with the *future tense* form of each verb. Where you see _____ (neg.) write the negative form of the verb.

Next year I _____ to college. I _____ English and
               go   study

_____ courses in math and science. I _____ for fifteen
   take   register

credits. It_____ easy, but I _____ hard and if I need help, I
            be (neg.)   work

_____ my teachers and my counselor. I _____ also
   ask

_____ a tutor. To pay for college, I_____ tuition assistance. I
   get   request

_____ also _____ for a bank loan. To cover my personal
                       apply

expenses, I _____ for a part time job. It_____ easy, but it
               look   be (neg.)

_____ worth it. Some day I _____ with a diploma and
   be   graduate

_____ a good job and a better life.
   have

112

A NUCLEAR WAR?

ACTIVITY   Read the story. Below are *answers* about the story. On the lines at the left write *questions* that go with each answer.

A pessimist predicts that the world will end by the year 2000. He says there will be a nuclear war between the United States and the Soviet Union. These countries will destroy each other and millions of people in other countries will die from radiation.

An optimist says this will not happen. The nuclear powers will agree to limit weapons and eventually they will disarm completely. They will not want to risk total destruction. There will be peace throughout the world by the year 2000.

Questions	*Answers*
1. _____ ?	In the year 2000.
2. _____ ?	Because of a nuclear war.
3. _____ ?	The U.S. and the Soviet Union.
4. _____ ?	Millions.
5. _____ ?	From radiation.
6. _____ ?	An optimist.
7. _____ ?	Yes, they will.
8. _____ ?	Disarm completely.
9. _____ ?	No, they won't.
10. _____ ?	Yes, there will.

PETE'S DAY

ACTIVITY   Read the story below. Fill in the blanks with the *future tense* form of each verb. Where you see _____ write the negative form of the verb.
(neg.)

Pete _____ time to see his girlfriend tomorrow. He _____
have (neg.)   be

busy all day and all night. In the morning he _____ his mother. She is an old woman
visit

and can't get around much anymore so Pete _____ the shopping for her. He
do

_____ also _____ her dog to the veterinarian. When he
take

finishes that, he _____ his car to the garage. There is something wrong with the
drive

transmission. He _____ for the car to be fixed. He _____
wait (neg.)   come back

later in the afternoon. He _____ to see a friend who owes him some money. Then he
go

_____ the train uptown to the office of his lawyer. He _____
take   talk

to his lawyer about some legal matters concerning some property he owns in New Jersey. The lawyer

_____ him some legal papers to sign. Pete _____ them with
give   take

him so that he can read them first. He _____ the lawyer that he
tell

_____ the papers back next week. After he finishes with his lawyer, he
send

_____ downtown and _____ his car at the garage. By this
return   pick up

time it _____ late afternoon. He _____ to the airport to pick
be   hurry

up a friend who is coming from Haiti.

He _____ his friend out to dinner. They _____ about old
take   talk

times. They _____ a pleasant evening together. Pete _____
spend   be (neg.)

sorry that he decided to see his friend again after all these years.

114

ACTIVITY Below are *answers* about the story, "Pete's Day." On the lines at the left write *questions* that go with each answer.

Questions   Answers

1. _____ ? No, he won't.

2. _____ ? Yes, he will.

3. _____ ? In the morning.

4. _____ ? Because she is an old woman.

5. _____ ? Later in the afternoon.

6. _____ ? His lawyer.

7. _____ ? By train.

8. _____ ? To the airport.

9. _____ ? Talk about old times.

10. _____ ? Yes, they will.

THE HOMEMAKER

ACTIVITY   Look at the picture on page 76. Then read the story below and fill in the blanks with the *future* tense of each verb. Where you see _____ write the negative form of the verb.
(neg.)

This little girl _____ with ideas about life that are different from those her
grow up

grandparents had. She _____ that women must stay home and that men must go
think (neg.)

out to work. She _____ than men and women can do many different things. If she
understand

wants to be a wife and mother, she _____ and _____ children. If
get married   have

she wants to have a career, she _____ her education and _____
finish   look

for a job. If she wants to have both a family and a career, she _____ a man who
marry

_____ her needs and _____ her meet them. They
recognize   help

_____ this before they get married. They _____ together how
discuss   plan

to work and have a family, and they _____ the responsibilities. They
share

_____ unpleasant chores on each other.
"dump" (neg.)

When this little girl grows up, she _____ wherever she wants to. She
live

_____ the things she wants in life and she _____ any regrets.
give up (neg.)   have (neg.)

ACTIVITY   Below are *answers* about the story. Write *questions* that go with each answer.

Questions	*Answers*
1. _____ ?	Yes, she will.
2. _____ ?	No, she won't.
3. _____ ?	That men and women can do many things.
4. _____ ?	She will get married and have children.
5. _____ ?	Because she wants to have a career.
6. _____ ?	A man who recognizes her needs.
7. _____ ?	Before they get married.
8. _____ ?	Yes, they will.
9. _____ ?	No, they won't.
10. _____ ?	Wherever she wants to.

THE FOOTBALL GAME

ACTIVITY   Read the story below and fill in the blanks with the *present continuous* form of each verb.

Right now I _____ a football game on television. Two good teams
                                                       watch

_____ . One team _____ , 7–0. The other team
    play   win

_____ any points. Now two players _____ . The referee
   get (neg.)   fight

_____ to break it up. The referee _____ a good job. The fans
    try   do (neg.)

_____ their team will win.
   hope

A LETTER

ACTIVITY   Read the letter below and fill in the blanks with the *present continuous* form of each verb.

888 First Avenue
Westwood, California
October 15, 19– –

Dear Ricardo,

    I _____ on a bench in my neighborhood park and _____
       sit   enjoy

the beautiful autumn weather here. The wind _____ and some leaves
                                      blow

_____ . I _____ to college now and I
   fall   go

_____ English. I _____ also _____ part
   study   work

time as an elevator operator.

    I _____ now _____ an apartment with my brother Tony
                              share

and his wife Sara. He _____ in a factory and she _____
                 work   attend

school. Together we _____ up the apartment in our spare time. Tony and Sara
               fix

_____ to go back home for a visit at Christmas, but I _____ . I
   plan   go (neg.)

_____ in the city and _____ it easy.
   stay   take

_____ you still _____ to school? What _____
                    go

you _____ to do at Christmas? Please write to me soon.
  hope

Your friend,
Nelson

THE TUBE BOOB

ACTIVITY   Look at the picture on page 74. Then read the story below and fill in the blanks with the *present continuous* form of each verb. Where you see _____ write the negative form of the verb.
                                                                                        (neg.)

This is the living room of an apartment. There _____ television sets

_____ all around the room. A lamp _____ on one television
              stand   rest

set, an empty coffee cup on another. One television set _____ on the sofa and
                                                                          lie

others _____ on the floor. There are even TV sets on top of TV sets. But they
                    rest

_____ .
       work (neg.)

There are three people in the apartment: Ed; Ed's wife, Mabel; and Mabel's friend Maryanne. Ed

_____ another TV set into the apartment. Mabel and Maryanne
              carry

_____ next to each other. Mabel _____ to Maryanne. Ed
           sit   talk

_____ a long cigar. Mabel _____ but Maryanne
              smoke   smile

_____ . She _____ to figure out what
       smile (neg.)   try

_____ on. Ed _____ anything to Mabel, but he
           go   say (neg.)

doesn't have to. Mabel understands what_____ and she_____
                                                     happen   begin

to explain the situation to Maryanne. What do you think she _____ ?
                                                                                  say

THE COUNTRY HOUSE

ACTIVITY Read the story. Below are *answers* about the story. On the lines at the left write *questions* that go with each answer.

Marjorie is sitting on the porch of her country house. No one is making a sound. Her mother is reading the paper. Her dog is sleeping. The TV set isn't playing. Her father is driving into town to buy groceries. Her husband and children are walking to the lake. They are coming home for lunch. The birds are singing and some insects are buzzing. The sun is shining. The wind is gently blowing the leaves. No cars are passing. Marjorie is feeling relaxed and peaceful. She isn't worrying about a thing. She is having a good time.

Questions	*Answers*
1. _____ ?	On the porch.
2. _____ ?	No.
3. _____ ?	Her mother.
4. _____ ?	Sleeping.
5. _____ ?	No, it isn't.
6. _____ ?	Into town.
7. _____ ?	To buy groceries.
8. _____ ?	To the lake.
9. _____ ?	For lunch.
10. _____ ?	Singing.
11. _____ ?	Buzzing.
12. _____ ?	Yes, it is.
13. _____ ?	Blowing the leaves.
14. _____ ?	No, they aren't.
15. _____ ?	Relaxed and peaceful.
16. _____ ?	No, she isn't.
17. _____ ?	Yes, she is.
18. _____ ?	In their country house.
19. _____ ?	The whole family.
20. _____ ?	In the summer.

BARROOM BRAWL

ACTIVITY   Look at the picture. Then read the story below and fill in the blanks with the *present continuous* form of each verb. Where you see _____ (neg.) write the negative form.

This incident _____ (take) place in a bar. All the patrons of the bar

_____ (have) a fight. They _____ (say (neg.)) anything. They

_____ just _____ (brawl) . One of the patrons

_____ (lean) back with his elbows on the bar. The man in front of him

_____ (grab) him with his right hand and _____ (threaten) to hit him with the

left.

Behind them a man and woman _____ (fight) . The woman _____ (swing)

her handbag and _____ (try) to hit him. The man _____ (lift) one of his

hands and _____ (hope) to defend himself. He probably _____ (go (neg.)) to hit

the woman.

To the right of the picture, two men _____ (hit) each other. One of the men

_____ (punch) the other one in the jaw. The man who _____ (be) punched

_____ (fall) over backward. His hat _____ (drop) off his head.

In front of them, two more men _____ (struggle) . One _____ (lie) on

his back on the floor. The other _____ (sit) on top of him. Their hats

_____ (rest) on the floor. Next to them another couple of men _____ (battle) .

One _____ (strangle) the other. They _____ (glare) at each other. While all of

this _____ (go) on, the bartenders _____ (stand) next to each other

behind the bar and _____ (talk) . They _____ (stop (neg.)) the fight. One

_____ (tell) the other how the fight started. What _____ he

_____ (say) ?

LOOKING OUT THE WINDOW

ACTIVITY Read the story below and fill in the blanks with the *present continuous* form of each verb. Where you see _____ write the negative form of the verb.
(neg.)

I _____ in my room and _____ out the window. A young
sit   look

couple _____ by. They _____ to each other. An old man
walk   talk (neg.)

_____ by. He _____ a heavy package. Here comes a
limp   carry

photographer. He _____ along a camera case and a tripod. He
drag

_____ pictures. Here comes a man who _____ a pink hat.
take (neg.)   wear

Cars and taxis _____ down the street. Now they _____ for a
drive   stop

red light. The light _____ green and they _____ again. It
turn   start

_____ but the cars' windshield wipers _____ . It
rain   move (neg.)

_____ to get dark. I _____ to work but my daughter
begin   try

_____ in the next room with a friend. They _____ quiet. Now
play   be (neg.)

I _____ hungry. I _____ work and _____
get   quit   go

in to eat.

ACTIVITY Below are *answers* about the story, "Looking Out the Window." On the lines at the left, write *questions* that go with each answer.

	Questions	Answers
1.	_____ ?	In my room.
2.	_____ ?	Looking out the window.
3.	_____ ?	A young couple.
4.	_____ ?	An old man.
5.	_____ ?	A heavy package.
6.	_____ ?	A camera case.
7.	_____ ?	A pink hat.
8.	_____ ?	Work.
9.	_____ ?	My daughter.
10.	_____ ?	I am.

THE TEACHER'S VIEW

ACTIVITY   Read the story below and fill in the blanks with the *present continuous* form of each verb. Where you see _____ (neg.) write the negative form of the verb.

I _____ sit _____ in front of the class. The students _____ work _____ . They

_____ write _____ a composition. Well, some of them _____ do _____ it, but others

_____ just _____ laugh _____ . Some students _____ do (neg.) _____

anything. They _____ stare _____ into space and _____ look _____ dumb. Maybe

they _____ try (neg.) _____ . Maybe they _____ sleep _____ . Some

_____ come (neg.) _____ to class at all. Freddy _____ fail _____ . Charlie

_____ pass (neg.) _____ either. The others _____ hope _____ to pass. I

_____ look _____ forward to the summer vacation.

ACTIVITY   Below are *answers* about the story, "The Teacher's View." On the lines at the left, write *questions* that go with each answer.

Questions	*Answers*
1. _____ ?	In front of the class.
2. _____ ?	Yes, they are.
3. _____ ?	A composition.
4. _____ ?	Just laughing.
5. _____ ?	Staring into space.
6. _____ ?	Maybe.
7. _____ ?	Freddy.
8. _____ ?	No, he isn't.
9. _____ ?	Pass.
10. _____ ?	The summer vacation.

TRAFFIC REPORTER

ACTIVITY   Read the story below and fill in the blanks with the *present continuous* form of each verb. Where you see _____ write the negative form of the verb.
(neg.)

This is your WINS traffic reporter. I _____ in helicopter 1010 and right now I
                                      fly

_____ over the West Side Highway. Traffic _____ slowly
         go   move

south but all vehicles _____ at normal speed going north. The George Washington
                              drive

Bridge _____ a heavy load at this moment, so if you _____ to
           carry   try

get into New York quickly, we _____ you to use the Lincoln Tunnel. Traffic
                                      advise

_____ good time on the FDR Drive south and it _____ over
      make (neg.)   crawl

the 59th Street Bridge. Cars _____ now at the entrance to the Holland Tunnel
                                   stop

because of a stalled vehicle in the left lane. It _____ to rain now but it
                                                          begin

_____ traffic. Traffic still _____ up at the Brooklyn-Battery
    affect (neg.)   clear (neg.)

Tunnel, but it _____ to move on the Brooklyn Bridge. This has been your WINS
                     start

traffic reporter, and I _____ off now.
                              sign

ACTIVITY   Below are *answers* about the story, "Traffic Reporter." On the lines at the left, write *questions* that go with each answer.

	Questions		*Answers*
1.	_____	?	A helicopter.
2.	_____	?	Over the West Side Highway.
3.	_____	?	Slowly going south and at normal speed going north.
4.	_____	?	The George Washington Bridge.
5.	_____	?	The Lincoln Tunnel.
6.	_____	?	No, it isn't.
7.	_____	?	Because of a stalled vehicle.
8.	_____	?	No, it isn't.
9.	_____	?	Yes, it is.
10.	_____	?	Signing off.

THE BANK ROBBERY

ACTIVITY   Read the story below and fill in the blanks with the *present continuous* form of each verb. Where you see _____ write the negative form of the verb.
(neg.)

I can't believe what _____ . Those four men _____ that
happen   rob

bank! One of them _____ a gun at a teller. He _____ her to
point   tell

put all the money in a bag. She _____ to open the drawer where the money is, but
try

she _____ with fear. The robber _____ nervous. The other
shake   get

tellers _____ anything. They _____ any chances. Another
do (neg.)   take (neg.)

robber _____ the security guard. The guard _____ to get
tie up   struggle

loose but the robber is stronger. The third robber _____ the bank customers in a
put

closet. The customers _____ . The fourth robber _____
resist (neg.)   pay (neg.)

attention to what _____ . He _____ near the door to make
go on   stand

sure that no one comes in.

ACTIVITY   Below are *answers* about the story, "The Bank Robbery." On the lines at the left write *questions* that go with each answer.

Questions	Answers
1. _____ ?	Yes, they are.
2. _____ ?	A gun.
3. _____ ?	To put all the money in a bag.
4. _____ ?	Yes, she is.
5. _____ ?	No, they aren't.
6. _____ ?	Yes, he is.
7. _____ ?	In a closet.
8. _____ ?	No, he isn't.
9. _____ ?	Near the door.
10. _____ ?	To make sure that no one comes in.

125

THE NEIGHBORHOOD

ACTIVITY   Read the story below and fill in the blanks with the *present continuous* form of each verb. Where you see _____ write the negative form of the verb.
(neg.)

Right now I _____ out of my bedroom window at the street. A lot of things
look

_____ in my neighborhood. Some young girls _____ rope on
happen   jump

the sidewalk. At the corner a man _____ ice cream from his truck. He
sell

_____ many customers because it is a cool day. Across the street two men
get (neg.)

_____ an argument. Directly above them a woman _____ at
have   shout

them to make them shut up. In the middle of the street five boys _____ ball. A man
play

in a green Chevy _____ to pass by. He _____ his horn at the
try   blow

boys, but they _____ any attention to him. A young boy _____
pay (neg.)   run

down the street. He _____ a small suitcase and a teddy bear. His mother
carry

_____ out of the building after him yelling, "Stop! Come home!" My neighbor
come

_____ his new car. His son _____ nearby, but he
wash   stand

_____ him. A teenage boy _____ on the front step of his
help (neg.)   lie

house across the street. He _____ to music on his radio. His two sisters
listen

_____ to the music. What a busy neighborhood!
dance

ACTIVITY   Below are *answers* about the story, "The Neighborhood." On the lines at the left, write *questions* that go with each answer.

	Questions		*Answers*
1.	_____ ?		Right now.
2.	_____ ?		Yes, there are.
3.	_____ ?		Some young girls.
4.	_____ ?		A man at the corner.
5.	_____ ?		Having an argument.
6.	_____ ?		Shouting at them.
7.	_____ ?		In the middle of the street.
8.	_____ ?		A man in a green Chevy.
9.	_____ ?		No, they aren't.
10.	_____ ?		A small suitcase and a teddy bear.
11.	_____ ?		"Stop! Come home!"
12.	_____ ?		Washing his new car.
13.	_____ ?		On the front step of his house.
14.	_____ ?		Listening to music.
15.	_____ ?		Dancing.

SUMMER PLANS

ACTIVITY   Read the story below and fill in the blanks with the appropriate form for each verb. Where you see _____ write the negative form of the verb. You will have to use *different tenses* in this exercise.   (neg.)

Next summer I _____ home. I _____ a little and
        stay   work

_____ a lot. I would _____ to _____ to
   play   like   go

Canada for a vacation. Five years ago I _____ in Canada and I
                                              be

_____ it very much. I _____ around a lot and
   enjoy   drive

_____ some wonderful meals. I _____ anywhere last year and
   eat   can go (neg.)

although now I _____ ready to _____ another trip, I just
                   be   take

_____ enough money. My wife _____ staying home either.
   have (neg.)   mind (neg.)

Her parents _____ to _____ us in July. We
                 come   visit

_____ some time at the beach and _____ to
   spend   go

_____ my parents in Texas.
   visit

HENRY AND ANITA

ACTIVITY   Read each part of the following story. Below each part are *answers*. On the lines at the left, write *questions* that go with each answer about the story. You will have to use *different tenses* throughout this activity.

Henry was born in Italy. He went to high school, but he doesn't have a diploma. He lives in the United States now. He is married to Anita. They were married in 1980.

Henry and Anita have one child named Sofia. Henry works in a store and earns $400 a week. He doesn't like his job. He wants to get a high school diploma.

Questions	Answers
1. _____?	Italy.
2. _____?	Yes, he did.
3. _____?	No, he doesn't.
4. _____?	In the United States.
5. _____?	Anita.
6. _____?	In 1980.
7. _____?	One child.
8. _____?	Sofia.
9. _____?	In a store.
10. _____?	$400 a week.

Now Henry is attending school at night. He isn't wasting his time. He is studying hard. He and his wife are saving their money. They are planning to buy a house in the future. They will move to the suburbs. Henry will get a different job. Anita will go back to school and get a diploma also. Then she will get a job. They will have a happy life.

Questions	Answers
11. _____?	Yes, he is.
12. _____?	No, he isn't.
13. _____?	Studying hard.
14. _____?	Saving their money.
15. _____?	Buy a house.
16. _____?	To the suburbs.
17. _____?	Yes, he will.

JOHN'S STORY

ACTIVITY Read the story below and fill in the blanks with the appropriate form for each verb. Where you see _____ write the negative form of the verb. You will have to use *different tenses* in this activity.

Last week John _____ two films and a show. He _____
                        see   have

dinner with a friend. He _____ a lot of television. He _____
                              watch   feel (neg.)

like doing much work. He _____ asleep every night.
                              fall

This week he _____ much better. Although he _____ his
                  look   like (neg.)

job, he _____ any trouble doing his work. He _____ full of
            have (neg.)   be

energy. He _____ to work. He _____ to bed early.
              walk   go (neg.)

Next week he _____ to get another job. He _____ in the
                  try   look

newspapers and _____ for interviews. He _____ lazy. He
                    go   be (neg.)

_____ to dinners and shows. His friends _____ proud of him.
  go (neg.)   be

He _____ .
      succeed

ACTIVITY Below are *answers* to "John's Story." On the lines at the left, write *questions* that go with each answer. You will have to use *different tenses* in this activity.

Questions	Answers
1. _____ ?	Two films and a show.
2. _____ ?	Last week.
3. _____ ?	No, he didn't.
4. _____ ?	Yes, he did.
5. _____ ?	No, he doesn't.
6. _____ ?	Yes, he is.
7. _____ ?	He walks.
8. _____ ?	Next week.
9. _____ ?	In the newspapers.
10. _____ ?	No, he won't.

PICTURE STORY 1 REVISITED

Form a group of 3 or 4 people. Look at the picture on page 73. Read the sentences describing the picture, and fill in the blanks with the *prepositions* that you and your group *agree on*. Choose from the list below.

in	to	around	under
on	next to	about	outside
at	opposite	between	through
with	across from	behind	against
of			

Decide on the words you want to use in no. 31. Think of a good title for the cartoon. Write it on the line below.

(Title) _____

1. The setting for this cartoon is a typical living room of an apartment _____ a large building _____ a big city.

2. The apartment is _____ the first or second floor _____ the building.

3. _____ the windows, we can see other apartment buildings.

4. _____ the room there are two couches _____ each other.

5. There is a coffee table _____ the two couches.

6. _____ the coffee table there are some flowers _____ a vase, and an ashtray.

7. There are some pictures _____ the walls.

8. There is a large plant _____ one picture and there are some bookshelves _____ the other picture.

9. There is a lamp _____ one of the couches.

10. There are four average-looking middle-aged people _____ the room and one weird-looking person _____ the room.

11. A dark-haired man _____ glasses is sitting _____ one couch.

12. He has a pipe _____ his mouth and a smile _____ his face.

13. He is holding a drink _____ his hand.

14. He is probably the husband _____ the woman _____ the print pants suit, who is holding a tray _____ some crackers and cheese _____ it.

15. She is the hostess and her husband is the host.

16. She has curly hair and a thin, pointed nose.

17. The woman is serving hors d' oeuvres _____ a man and woman who are sitting _____ the couch which is _____ their host.

18. The woman's arm is resting _____ the arm _____ the couch.

19. Her legs are crossed and she is balancing a cocktail glass _____ her lap.

20. She is wearing a dark dress _____ a polka-dot scarf _____ her neck.

21. Her companion is sitting _____ her.

22. He is holding a drink _____ his left hand.

23. Both _____ them are looking _____ the hostess.

24. They have worried, puzzled expressions _____ their faces.

25. They are probably wondering _____ the strange-looking sight _____ the window.

26. A rather heavy, bald man is standing _____ a ladder, which is leaning _____ the window.

27. He is wearing a mask _____ angry-looking eyes and big teeth.

28. His big hands are _____ his head with the thumbs stuck _____ his ears, and he is waving his hands as if he is trying to scare the guests.

29. But the hostess does not seem to be worried.

30. She is smiling and saying something _____ her guests.

31. Maybe she is talking about the man, and maybe she isn't. What do you think she is saying? Put her words here:

"_____

_____."

CHIN'S FRUIT STORE

PRONOUNS

Subject	Object	Possessive Adjectives	Reflexive
I	me	my	myself
you	you	your	yourself
he	him	his	himself
she	her	her	herself
it	it	its	itself
we	us	our	ourselves
they	them	their	themselves

In the spaces below, fill in the correct *pronouns* from the list above.

Micky Chin owns a fruit store on Main Street. _____ and _____ wife, Laura, and

_____ son, David, work in the store every day of the week. _____ work very hard. Micky

goes to the fruit and vegetable market by _____ early each morning to buy what _____

needs. Laura opens the store at seven. _____ arranges the merchandise and gets ready for the

early morning customers. _____ always smiles and talks to _____ . The customers smile

back at_____ . Laura works by _____ until 8 o'clock. Then_____ mother comes

to help. Micky arrives with the produce by 8:30 and the three of _____ arrange_____ on

the stalls and shelves. _____ do a lot of business in the morning and also late in the afternoon.

David arrives from school about 2 P.M. and Micky tells _____ what to do. Laura and

_____ mother go home at 7 P.M. and Micky and _____ son stay by _____ .

_____ close the store at midnight.

_____ fruit store is very successful. When Micky came from Korea five years ago with

_____ family, _____ had very little money. Now_____ is doing very well. Micky

says, "_____ family and _____ work very hard. _____ don't have much time to

relax and enjoy _____ . But soon_____ will hire some people to help _____ and

_____ lives will be easier. This country has been good to _____ . If you work hard and

help _____ , _____ dreams can come true."

REVIEW EXERCISE 1

Pronouns: he, she, him, her, his, her, they, them, their
Prepositions: at, on, in, for, of, to, from, with

A.   In the spaces below, fill in the correct *prepositions* from the list above.

Mary was born _____ Ohio _____ 5 P.M. _____ January 21, 1955. She lived

_____ her parents and one sister named Janice. They lived _____ 221 Columbus

Avenue. Later they lived _____ Marion Street. However, she spent most _____ her

childhood _____ Latin America because her father was _____ the construction business

and he was building highways. Mary and her sister went _____ private schools and they got a very

good education. _____ course, they both spoke Spanish fluently.

B.   In the spaces below, fill in the correct *pronouns* from the list above.

Mary had dark hair and a very pretty face. _____ eyes were brown and large and

_____ teeth were white and even. _____ always weighed too much, though, and didn't

have many boyfriends. _____ sister Janice, on the other hand, was slender and blonde and very

lovely. All the boys liked _____ , and _____ used to go out on a lot of dates.

When Mary finished high school, _____ parents moved back to the United States and

_____ went to college. _____ studied languages and was a very good student.

_____ didn't have many dates in college either and _____ life wasn't so happy. But

_____ had a very pleasant personality, and people liked _____ very much.

C.   Fill in the correct *prepositions*.

When Mary graduated _____ college she applied _____ a job _____

Washington working _____ the government. She went _____ Washington _____

June 1976. _____ Washington she met three young women who were also just starting to work

_____ her agency, and they decided to share a house. One _____ the women was

_____ New Jersey and she had a friend named Richard who was also working there. Mary met

Richard and fell _____ love _____ him.

D. Fill in the correct *prepositions* and *pronouns* in the spaces below.

Richard liked Mary. _____ (pron.) went out together _____ (prep.) three months and had a very

good time. _____ (prep.) the end _____ (prep.) three months, the agency told Mary that _____ (pron.)

was going to send _____ (pron.) _____ (prep.) the Philippines. _____ (pron.) told Richard that

_____ (pron.) wouldn't go if _____ (pron.) didn't want _____ (pron.) to, but _____ (pron.) told

_____ (pron.) to go. _____ (pron.) planned to go back _____ (prep.) New Jersey and work _____ (prep.)

_____ (pron.) father's business.

E. Fill in the correct *pronouns*.

_____ last night together was very romantic for _____ . _____ went out to a

good French restaurant and then _____ took _____ back to _____ apartment for

champagne. _____ promised _____ would write to each other and _____ gave

_____ a music box that played one of _____ favorite songs, "La Mer." _____ gave

_____ a book of love poems. _____ both cried when _____ said goodbye.

F. In the blanks below, fill in the correct form of the verb in the *past tense*. Where you see _____ (neg.)
    write in the negative form of the verb.

Two weeks after Mary _____ (arrive) in Manila, she _____ (meet)

Tony. A colleague at the American embassy where she _____ (work) ,

_____ (take) her to a little bar in the old part of the city. Tony _____ (be)

playing guitar with a small band and throughout the evening he _____ (smile) at her and

_____ (seem) to be playing just for her. Mary _____ (keep) drinking rum-

and-cokes and feeling sorry for herself. She _____ (miss) Richard very much. During a

break, Tony _____ (come) to her table and _____ (ask) if he

_____ (can) play a song for her. She _____ (tell) him to play "La Mer."

He _____ (play) it and she _____ (cry) .

A week later, Mary _____ (go) back alone to the bar. When Tony

_____ (see) her he _____ (sing) "La Mer." Later he

_____ (sit) down with her and _____ (buy) her a drink she never

_____ (have) before _____ (call) a Mai Tai. She _____ (like)

it very much. She also _____ to like Tony. Soon she _____

start
be

going to the bar almost every night, and after a while Tony _____ playing "La Mer"

stop

and _____ playing his favorite song, "El Reloj." Then they _____

start
go

out together. Although Mary _____ Richard, she _____ in

forget (neg.)
fall

love with Tony.

  Tony _____ very nice to her, but they _____ much time

be
have (neg.)

together; they only _____ each other during the week. It _____

see
matter (neg.)

to her; she _____ to marry him.

want

  After Mary had been in Manila for six months, she _____ out she

find

_____ pregnant. When she _____ Tony, he

be
tell

_____ he _____ marry her because he

say
can (neg.)

_____ already married. Mary _____ what to do. She

be
know (neg.)

_____ of killing herself. She _____ of having an abortion. But

think
think

then she finally _____ to keep the baby and go back home.

decide

G. In the spaces below, fill in the correct form of the verbs in the *present continuous*. Where you see
_____ write in the negative form of the verb.

(neg.)

  Now Mary _____ in Virginia just outside Washington. She

live

_____ still _____ for the government and

work

_____ to be a good mother to her little girl Kay. Kay is three years old and she

try

_____ and _____ . Kay _____ to

walk
talk
go

nursery school. Mary _____ a lot of responsibility. She _____

carry
support

herself and her daughter by working all day and she _____ care of Kay at night.

take

Mary _____ out on dates but she has friends. They _____

go (neg.)
be

good to her and they _____ for a nice man for her to go out with. But they

look

_____ any luck. There is only one bright spot in her life. She

have (neg.)

_____ to Richard.

write

H. In the spaces below, fill in the correct form of the verbs in the *simple present* tense.

Richard still _____ in New Jersey and _____ for his
         live   work

father. He _____ a lot of money. He _____ married. He
     make   be (neg.)

_____ now he _____ ready to get married. That
  think   be

_____ why he _____ to Mary. He _____
 be   write   mind (neg.)

that she _____ a little girl. He _____ to see them both.
    have   want

Mary's friends _____ she should see him again. They _____
      think (neg.)   say

he _____ a good man. They _____ her he
  be (neg.)   tell

_____ to be the right person for her. They _____ her to find
 seem (neg.)   want

someone else. They _____ afraid she will get hurt again. They
       be

_____ questions about him, but Mary _____ those
 have   have (neg.)

questions. She _____ happy memories of her time with Richard. She
     have

_____ to see him soon.
 hope

REVIEW EXERCISE 2

A. Fill in the missing *prepositions* in the spaces below.

Denise Graves was born _____ March 24, 19— _____ Cleveland, Ohio. Until she

was two-and-a-half she lived _____ her parents and two sisters _____ 338 W. Bellevue

Street. _____ 10 o'clock _____ the morning, _____ a Saturday _____

September 19—, she was kidnapped by Harold Gross while she was playing_____ the backyard

_____ her house. Gross took the girl _____ his parents who lived _____ a farm

_____ Buffalo, N.Y. and told them that she was his child. Gross had a brother named Daniel, who

lived _____ the same street as the Graves family.

B. Fill in the missing *pronouns* in the spaces below.

Right after the kidnapping, Mr. Graves, the girl's father, went on television to ask for_____

daughter's return. _____ begged the kidnapper to bring_____ back. _____ said

that_____ was not healthy and that_____ needed medicine. Mr. and Mrs. Graves were

very upset. _____ offered a reward of $10,000 for the return of _____ daughter. Many

people called _____ to give advice. Mrs. Graves thought _____ would never see

_____ daughter again. Mr. Graves was so upset _____ killed himself. The police found

_____ dead in_____ garage near the tailpipe of_____ automobile. _____

said _____ died of carbon monoxide poisoning.

C. Fill in the correct form of the verbs below in the *past* tense.

Two years later, Daniel Gross_____ Denise and _____
                                       see   call
the police. He _____ he _____ her because he had been a
                    say   know
friend of the girl's father. Mr. and Mrs. Gross, who were taking care of Denise, _____
                                                                                          be
arrested. The Cleveland police _____ Mrs. Graves to Buffalo and she
                                       take
_____ her daughter. When the mother_____ at the girl she
        identify   look
_____ down and_____ . Then she _____
        fall   scream   run
to her and _____ her. She _____ crying when the little girl
                  hug   start
_____ her. Mrs. Graves _____ Denise back to Cleveland but
   recognize (neg.)   bring

138

the girl _____ her own name. The mother, who had just married again,
_____remember (neg.)_____

_____ when reporters _____ her how she
_____cry_____ _____ask_____

_____ . "I never _____ hoping I _____
_____feel_____ _____stop_____ _____will_____

see her again," she _____ . She _____ the reporters that she
_____reply_____ _____tell_____

_____ angry with the kidnapper, but the sisters _____ that
_____be (neg.)_____ _____shout_____

they _____ to kill him.
_____want_____

D. Fill in the correct form of the verbs below in the *present* tense.

Now the little girl _____ home with her family. She _____
_____be_____ _____know_____

her sisters and she _____ her new father, but she _____ her
_____like_____ _____remember (neg.)_____

real father. The sisters _____ happy to have her back and they
_____be_____

_____ good care of her. The mother _____ , "I _____
_____take_____ _____say_____ _____be_____

so happy. I _____ what to do first. I _____ . I
_____know (neg.)_____ _____can think (neg.)_____

_____ going to lose her again."
_____be (neg.)_____

Denise _____ blond hair and a light complexion. "_____
_____have_____ _____call (neg.)_____

me Denise," she _____ her mother because she _____ her
_____tell_____ _____think_____

name _____ Susan. The mother _____ , "We
_____be_____ _____say_____

_____ . We _____ her Susan Denise."
_____compromise_____ _____call_____

E. Below are answers for questions about the story. Write an appropriate question for each answer.

Questions	Answers
1 _____?	Cleveland, Ohio.
2. _____?	September, 19—
3. _____?	$10,000.
4. _____?	Yes, he did.
5. _____?	No, she wasn't.
6. _____?	Medicine.
7. _____?	That she would never see her again.
8. _____?	Because he was a friend of her father's.
9. _____?	"I don't know what to do first."
10. _____?	Susan Denise.